Marketing Strategy for Authors

By

Tao Wong

Copyright

All rights reserved. No part of this publication may be reproduced in any form, or by any means, electronic or mechanical, including photocopying, recording, or any information browsing, storage, or retrieval system, without permission in writing from the author.

This book is licensed for your personal use only. This e-book may not be re-sold or given away to other people. If you would like to share this e-book with another person, please purchase an additional copy for each recipient. If you're reading this book and did not purchase it, or it was not purchased for your use only, then please return to your favourite e-book retailer and purchase your own copy. Thank you for respecting the hard work of this author.

Although this book is designed to provide accurate information in regard to the subject matter covered, the author assumes no responsibility for errors, inaccuracies, omissions, or any other inconsistencies herein. This publication is meant as a source of valuable information for the reader, however it is not meant as a replacement for direct expert assistance. If such level of assistance is required, the services of a competent professional should be sought.

Marketing Strategy for Authors

Copyright © 2020 Tao Wong. All rights reserved.

A Tao Wong Book
Published by Starlit Publishing
69 Teslin Rd
Whitehorse, YT
Y1A 3M5
Canada

www.mylifemytao.com

Ebook ISBN: 978-1-989994-43-6
Print ISBN: 978-1-989994-48-1

Contents

INTRODUCTION 1

DEVELOPING YOUR MARKETING PLAN 3
- GOALS 4
- ENVIRONMENT/INDUSTRY 5
- WORD OF WARNING 8
- THE 'I WRITE WHAT I WRITE' JUSTIFICATION 9
- USING THE INFORMATION & SOME CAVEATS 10
- MARKETING PLAN KPIs 11
- BUDGET 12
- RANDOM SAMPLE MARKETING BUDGET 16

THE FIRST P OF MARKETING: PRODUCT 19
- CHOOSING YOUR PRODUCT 20
- MAKING DECISIONS STRATEGICALLY 26
- THE PRODUCT LIFE CYCLE 28
- GROWTH SHARE MATRIX FOR WRITING 35
- PRODUCT LINE MANAGEMENT 40
- TO SERIES OR NOT? 41
- OTHER PRODUCT CONSIDERATIONS – RELEASE SPEED ... 43

THE SECOND P OF MARKETING: PRICING 45
- PREMIUM PRICING 45
- PRICE SKIMMING 46
- PENETRATION PRICING 47
- COST-PLUS PRICING 48
- COMPETITIVE PRICING 48
- PRICE DISCRIMINATION 49
- TIME-BASED PRICING 50

- Captive Product Pricing 51
- Promotional Pricing 51
- Bundle Pricing 52
- Anchor Pricing 53
- Kindle Unlimited (KU) 54
- Making Pricing Decisions as an Indie Publisher 55

THE THIRD P OF MARKETING: PLACEMENT 57

- Your Target Market 58
- The Breakdown 59
- A Brief Note on Print Distribution 60
- The Exclusive Option 64
- Going Wide 69
- Direct Sales 73

THE FOURTH P OF MARKETING: PROMOTION 75

- Above the Line Promotions 75
- Below the Line Promotions 76
- Sales Funnel 77
- The 10% Rule 78
- Understanding your Customers 79
- The Rule of 7 80
- Promotional Calendar 84
- The Basic Promotional Toolbox 87
- More Advanced Promotional Options 92
- Other Promotional Tools 96
- Promotional Plan Development Steps 102

EXAMPLES 105

- Bob 105

SUE	109
MANJIT	112
XIU LI	116
AFTERWORD	**119**
FURTHER READING	**121**
ABOUT THE AUTHOR	**127**
ABOUT THE PUBLISHER	**128**

Introduction

Who am I to write this book? No one really. I'm an extremely lucky indie author who stumbled onto initial success who then parlayed that success into an on-going full-time writing career. At the time of writing of this introduction, I have over twenty (20) books published, more than 1.5 million words in-print, most of my books having audiobooks, a comic series and multiple translations. Overall, I have over 50+ different product types (translations, shorts, anthologies, novels, novellas, audiobooks, comics, etc.).

If I had to say one thing that separates me from the vast majority of indie authors, it is that I have a grounding in both business and marketing. I ran a small business for over thirteen years as a sole proprietor, making it one of the largest retail businesses of its kind in Canada before I turned to writing full-time. I also worked as a marketing professional for many years beforehand after graduating with my MSc in Marketing from the University of Manchester.

But really, the reason I wrote this work is because it bothered me that so many discussions about 'marketing' among indie publishers and writers focused more on promotion than true marketing. There was a clear lack of understanding about general marketing theory and how it related to publishing.

And that lack not only impaired individual book launches, but long-term career choices.

So, I wrote this book to give an overview about basic (and this is super basic) marketing theory as it pertains to publishing.

At the end of this book, you should have an idea about how marketing theory relates to your own publishing career. It should provide guides to thinking, and prompt you to ask questions about where you are and how to make it to the next level of your publishing career.

Developing Your Marketing Plan

Building a marketing plan is a big, involved process. It's more complicated than most people think, and much of the processes we're looking at can be simplified for most independent authors. The simple fact is that as an individual business owner, few of you have the time to spend writing out a full marketing plan and updating it every six months.

As such, look at the following book as a guide for your thinking, as questions to ask yourself and an overall map to reach your goals. You do have to have a goal, and the more defined it is, the better. But the exact strategy and tactics involved will vary as you put all of this into practise.

The structure of this book is set up in the general way you'd build a marketing plan. The first chapter will help you define your goals, the development and analysis of your environment, and finally, what your marketing budget would be.

From there, we'll tackle the basic Four Ps of marketing: Product, Price, Place (Distribution) and finally, Promotion.

Lastly, we'll provide some basic examples of how to pull it all together so you have an understanding of how it all relates to one another.

Goals

Your own personal goals will dictate your marketing goals, which will influence your marketing plan. Because of that, it's hard to develop a full marketing plan template that can be useful for everyone. It's also worth noting that some of this is going to change based on what you sell because fiction and non-fiction are different beasts.

I'm going to use the goal of becoming a long-term, full-time author as the example. So, the marketing goal is (eventually) making, we'll call it, $50k a year. Let's assume you're starting out now, so there's no expectation to hit that $50k this year. But, let's assume you want to do it in 3 years. That means you'll need to scale up.

Now, we're beginning to have to hit a lot of assumptions while going through this process.

These assumptions include things like:

- Capital available for advertising
- Capital for product development

- Speed of product development (how fast do you write, edit and release!)
- Knowledge of social media outlets
- Advertising platform knowledge & capability
- Author physical location
- Whether you are an introvert or extrovert (and in-person sales ability!)

Whatever your situation may be with respect to the above points, you should be setting your marketing goals in a clear, trackable format for at least 3 years out. That might get longer if you write 1 book a year. This plan might be a 20-year plan.

Environment/Industry

Before you begin to even think about developing the marketing strategy, it's worth noting you need to have a clear understanding of the environment/industry before you start. Yes, you can stumble around without knowing what is going on. But if you don't know the terrain you're fighting in, you're just as likely to lose the war as you would by not knowing yourself or your enemy.

If you're a corporation (or have taken management classes); they tell you to use the SWOT (Strength, Weaknesses, Opportunities & Threat) analysis. Regarding external considerations, you can break it out further and use the PEST (Politics, Economic, Social

& Technological changes) analysis specific to the environment that you are working in. You can learn more about these analyses online, but in general these are fairly straightforward concepts.

I will say the one thing people always miss with the Strength/Weakness part of a SWOT analysis is that it is a **relative** analysis. **It is your strength or weakness compared to your competitors.**

In our case, it doesn't matter if you are a good writer, unless you are (by far) the best writer in your specific niche. And that's something to consider: how 'big' do you want to make this analysis? If you are doing write to market work; you need to analyse the whole industry. If you are a dedicated Sci-fi/Fantasy writer, maybe you only need to concern yourself with those writers. And even then, maybe it's best to look closer within your niche, such as at indie authors only or indie authors who have published in the last year.

What you want to do is make this **useful**. Putting together this analysis will help guide you to develop your marketing plan – whose goal, in our case, is to make money. So, reviewing the entire market might make no sense, unless you're planning to skip between genres and the like.

Some things to consider when you are looking at the above:

- Number of competitors and the number of increases in those competitors
- Platforms and platform types: web serial websites like Wattpad, Royal Road, etc.; retailers like Amazon, Kobo, B&N, Scribd, etc.
- Cover types and cover costs/value: how professional are the people you're looking to hire? What are the expectations specific to your genre?
- Trends and their rate of change (I'm looking at you, romance. But this also holds true for urban fantasy or paranormal romance where vampires might be out and werewolves in, magical academies are the hottest thing for this second, etc.).
- Competitor pricing
- Writing competency, generic tropes, tropes in demand, book length (basically, the product analysis of competitors)
- News outlets & social media hubs (e.g. LitRPG is really focused on a few Facebook groups and Reddit. There is not much in terms of reviews. Epic fantasy has a large number of dedicated blogs and reviewers that can help get the word out. etc.)
- Industry tech trends (AI voice recordings, audiobook growth, etc.)
- Speed of releases/release strategies

Once you've done that, we can start looking at building out the strategy aspects of your marketing plan.

Word of Warning

I see this happen a lot with people who have lots of school experience and/or have worked in Fortune 500 (or other very large) companies. They build out these elaborate 50-page documents, thinking that is what is necessary. As a small business entrepreneur, it is likely only you (and maybe your spouse or one other person) that is ever going to read your document. So, why bother creating something super professional?

Remember, the point of all these models, all this analysis is to **guide your thinking and research**. It is to force you to look at things that you might not have considered. It is not to make you sit there, wasting time because you have a box to fill. The more experienced you get, the less likely you will actually need a formal document. Nearly all the actual (start-up) entrepreneurs I know, who go on and do multiple businesses don't bother with big, formal documents like this, unless they're seeing banks or looking for funding (which as an author you are unlikely to ever get).

So. Do the work but do it so that you understand the environment and yourself. Not because you think it needs to be done up nicely and professionally for… something.

The 'I Write What I Write' Justification

Maybe you don't care what everyone else is writing, you write what you write because it's what you have to do. And this is where the 'art' side of publishing and writing comes in. I **know** that I should write 120-150k word books for LitRPG. I'd earn more in audiobooks and KU, readers prefer longer books in general. I don't write that, because I naturally peter out at 90-110k. I could add more words, but it would be 'wrong' for the books. I know that, and that's a trade-off I'm willing to make because I know my books are better off the way they are now than they would be if I extended them for a few dollars more.

Knowing the tropes is more to see what clicks for you than because you should 'check the tropes off'. It will also help you figure out how to market your books to the groups and people who want the stories you are telling. I am not telling you to write to trend, though if you can do that and do it well, great.

At the same time, if you are a natural writer, it's likely you have dozens of ideas buzzing in your head. Part of product marketing strategy can be as simple as choosing to write the ideas you have that will sell better at this moment.

If you are somewhat like me and just write what you do, the product analysis side of this can be a lot shorter. You will be looking at things like where they market, cover types, distribution locations and pricing. Stuff outside that can be ignored for the most part since you are just not going to do it, anyway.

As always, do what you need to do to keep writing.

Just realise that choices have consequences and that there are trade-offs.

Using the Information & Some Caveats

The next step is putting your plan together. This is kind of put together because your goals are going to have to change a little based on your budget and your analysis.

Again, a lot of this is going to be fuzzy if you are a new writer – and getting 'good' data is going to be hard. That's because one of the biggest question marks (your product) is very, very hard to evaluate as a new writer. Heck, even experienced writers have a hard time judging their own work. So, you won't know very well how you do in terms of writing and ability and how it compares until you publish.

This means that understanding how fast you can generate revenue is going to be hard. Which is why, again, I advise that you don't spend too much time on environmental analysis and the like. It's good to know what's going on, but until you publish and start marketing, it's hard to know what you're doing. We'll talk about reiteration and adaptation of the marketing plan later, but in the meantime, realise that you'll probably need to revise numbers.

Marketing Plan KPIs

That being said, assuming you have a 3-year goal, you should break your financial goals up now. In addition, it's time to start measuring – and considering how you measure – other Key Performance Indices (KPIs).

Here are some things you can measure:

- Organic Facebook fan page likes (please don't buy likes. Nothing from Fiverr or any of those mass purchases work).
- Newsletter subscribers (organic and swapped/promoed)
- Number of books released & types
- Number of short stories published
- Earned revenue

I'm sure you can think of more that works for your own situation.

Remember, make sure the KPIs are measurable and make sense for the business. Measuring Twitter followers might make sense, but measuring how many retweets a meme gets that has nothing to do with your writing probably doesn't. Unless you can measurably track back sales from those retweets, it might not be the best option. It certainly isn't a high-level KPI.

Note – I'm not measuring words written. Just published. You can't earn money if you don't publish. Then again, this goal is to earn 50k. Your goals might be different. You should adjust accordingly.

Budget

Now that you have an idea of the environment, it is time to play around with your budget. In an ideal world, you'd write your budget based on what you need to make, and then find the money to spend it. It's not an ideal world. It is also, in many ways, not a good idea to spend limited marketing dollars on advertising a single book. It is better to wait for more books to spend your advertising dollars on to gain a better return on investment (ROI).

Another thing to note is that your marketing budget is going to be dependent on your entire business budget. If you have $5000 to spend in a year and need to release 4 books, that money is likely better off spent in the most part on cover design and editing. If you have $6000, you might be able to break off a $1000 to do Facebook advertising and AMS (Amazon Marketing Services) ad testing. Or you could decide to put that money into an audiobook instead.

Which option you choose will depend on your marketing goals, your current KPIs (including unit sales of your e-book) and your timeframe. Can you wait until you get your audiobook out? Are your sales so low that you are missing the majority of readers with your e-book? Do you need to expand to a new market because you are 'reaching' the majority of your low-hanging fruit in e-books? Or maybe you just want your books in libraries, which means you need hardcovers and paperbacks. For Americans, that means paying for ISBNs.

Producing more products (of your own book) is a valid strategy, but it will affect your budget. Whether you decide to call it a production cost or a marketing cost, as a small business, it's all coming out of the same pot. So, it's worth working your marketing budget in view of your entire budget for the business.

Another thing to consider. Once you've created the budget, you might realise:

- You don't have enough money to cover basic production
- You don't have money to cover marketing

- You have enough money, but that's only because it's based on estimated sales for books not released.

In those cases, you might want to:

- Readjust your cost (can you release without three rounds of editing? Can you swap services?)
- Or increase your budget via non-author activities (can you sell your blood/plasma? Can you take a 2nd job or run errands? Kill your cable subscription so you can save money?)

Remember, this is a living document. You are better off estimating for a lower number of sales and revising upwards than estimating for a higher number of sales and revising downwards. This is, particularly, important for things like production budgets for your book (i.e. producing a low-quality series of books with bad covers is going to impact your sales more than throwing another $1000 at Facebook ads).

At this point, you have a budget. Most of that budget will be a bunch of made-up numbers (expenses should be firm, revenue will all be guesstimates until you produce and sell book one); but at least you've got something.

The Micro Budget Dilemma

What if you don't have much money at all? What if you have, say, $500 for your entire business? Or $200? What if you still intend to be an independent/self-published author with that amount of funds?

In almost all those cases, I'd recommend you ignore paid promotion. Your budget will be better spent producing a better work (cover, editing, proofing, etc.) than in paying for promotions. Cut out expenses that are not strictly necessary (e.g. developmental editing, ISBNs) and focus on releasing more work. You can get cheap pre-made covers that look professional for under $100, and you can find proofers that will work for as little as $0.003 per word.

Focus on production.

There are a few reasons for this:

- The more you write, and the more focused you are on learning from mistakes while writing, the better storyteller you become. The better storyteller you are, the more fans you'll gain, which allow each book to build upon the next.

> - It is very, very hard to get a positive ROI with only one (1) book released. General rule of thumb is three (3) books released in a series or nine (9) standalone books released before you expect to make money on paid promotional efforts. Again, there are ways to short-circuit this, but that's a good rule of thumb.
> - Lastly, with more books released (especially in a series); you have more options to drive eventual sales and returns (e.g. permafree books to entice new readers).

Random Sample Marketing Budget

Here's a random marketing budget that I pulled out of the air. This is just to give you an idea of what you could be doing and what your money could be spent on.

Year One:

- Budget: $500
- Tasks: Domain, website hosting, website creation, mailing list integration, some minor dollars thrown into AMS ads to increase visibility without breaking the bank.

- End of year goal: four books out, money from year one has hit the bank (including book three)

Year Two:

- Budget: $5000
- Tasks: Regular FB ads at a few dollars a day. AMS ads for first in series' and latest release. Newsletter marketing (Bookbub, Book Barbarian, etc.). Giveaways and contests on FB page. Produce book 1 or 2 of your series in audiobook. Produce paperback copies.
- End of year goal: eight books total released (four written in this year)

Year Three:

- Budget: $10,000
- Tasks: $10,000 in year 3 – Regular FB ads at $10-20 a day, AMS ads for multiple series. Regular newsletter marketing. Paying for newsletter subscribers now. Payment to go to a local con and sit at a table to meet fans. Put entire series into audiobook. Put entire series into hardcover.
- End of year goal: twelve books total released (four more in this year

The First P of Marketing: Product

Product is what you're selling. Without a product, you have nothing. Without a product, whether it's a course, a non-fiction book, your YouTube channel or a paperback, there's nothing to say. I'm setting aside the obvious question about your 'product' as an indie author, which is the quality (i.e. the craft component) of your writing as something that will not be discussed here. There are other people more qualified to listen to on that and is, frankly, impossible to evaluate in a book.

Suffice to say, you need a well written (as far as your genre is concerned) book to sell. What is considered well-written or good will vary from genre-to-genre. What might seem like dreck at first glance might be extremely popular for reasons that, you as an external reader / not in the genre, might not understand. You might not even understand why it's popular even if you are a reader in that genre because your taste is subtly different – or your craft level is not high enough to understand what the writer is doing.

I'm not touching discussions on what is 'good' or literary. I'm just assuming you have a product to sell in this section of the book.

Choosing your Product

You might not have much choice on what product to market. You might only have one book, one idea. Nothing wrong with that. Skip ahead further down.

Otherwise, there's a step before all this where you consider the kind of book/series/etc. that you want to write. This might be something to consider or dig into (i.e. do research on what sells) if you are, like many writers I know, filled with ideas. If you have a half-dozen ideas that you're equally interested in, there's nothing wrong with choosing the one that'll make you the most money. There are other books that discuss how to find a good genre to write in. The research methods constantly change, so it'd date this book if I tried to tackle it. For that matter, writing for magazines, shorts, etc. is a form of product choice. Remember, there's an *opportunity cost* involved in writing shorts or flash fiction or your non-fiction book or your fiction series. Time spent working on one thing is time not spent working on another project.

At least, until we learn time travel.

Here are some other things to consider when creating a product:

- Format presentation (certain mediums dictate your writing – e.g. contrast how webnovel serials, comics, novels and movie scripts are all different)
- Length of your work (flash fiction, novella, short story, novel, epic fantasy)
- Appendix, glossaries, images and additional material
- Speed of your writing/completion of work

Non-Book Products

We are getting into a longer talk about formats (and licensing), where you can potentially push your product (that initial idea, that initial universe) into multiple areas that aren't directly related to publishing.

For example, your product could be:

- A movie
- An anime
- A YouTube series
- A podcast
- Merchandised bookmarks, posters, t-shirts, toys,
- A musical (and the CD soundtrack, which is another product)
- Comics

- And on, and on, and on.

There's a whole book to be written about such things, and frankly, I'm not qualified to discuss most of it. So, I just want to leave that niggle in your brain that just because I'm talking of books here, it doesn't mean you can't do other forms of products from that initial idea.

Book Products

Now, let's assume you wrote a book. Not a comic, not a movie script, but a book. There's still a large question to ask, which is what kind of product format you want to make it. Here's a few of the most common suggestions (and again, remember, there are other product types that might make sense). Also, realise that each product type can cannibalise sales from other product types (e.g. having a paperback might take away from your e-book sales a little); but they also introduce you to a new market.

E-books

There are two major file formats for e-books – EPUB (used in iBooks, Kobo, Scribd, Amazon, etc.) and MOBI (Amazon exclusive but being deprecated). You might have also heard Kindle Unlimited (KU) mentioned, but that's not a format, that's a distribution method. We'll talk about it later on, when we get into the discussion of distribution. E-books are how most of us make our money as indie authors. They make up a large percentage of our income, anywhere from 60-99% (if you include KU which is delivered in e-book format).

Producing an e-book is a non-question if you have written a book these days. You can and should produce one.

Here's what you need to consider when producing an e-book:

1. Inclusion of images/appendices/etc. can affect your margin. Amazon can and will charge you more for larger books. Other retailers do not do so.
2. Formatting for e-books is different than for print.
3. This is often the 'base' form for most indie publishers. Every other format comes from here, and so the base production cost – editing, proofing, etc. is often assigned to this product.

Audiobooks

This is one of the fastest growing markets for publishing. Certain genres are heavily invested in audiobooks. The biggest concern about audiobooks is the high cost of production. As a rough estimate, using the audiobook narrator cost and including mastering and proofing cost, an audiobook will cost you US$350 per finished hour (PFH). There are approximately 9,300 words per finished hour, so a 60,000 word book will cost US$2,258 to produce. This is not including the prior cost of editing that has been assigned to e-books (i.e. developmental editing, line editing, etc.).

There are other methods of financing audiobooks (including royalty share with your narrators or sale of your audiobook rights which make alternative methods of providing them available, but are dependent to some extent upon your e-book sales and time and effort in finding narrators/producers.

To note, there's been a major indication that there might be a sea change in the audiobook market as AI voices come into play. It's *just* starting (as of 2020), but it's possible that in the next year or two; AI voices could become acceptable at most audiobook distributors. This would drive the cost of audiobook production down significantly. Another thing to note, is that audiobooks currently cost significantly more (for the consumer) than e-books. As production costs drop, expect the margin and the price to drop, too. Audiobooks are still anywhere from 1/5th to 1/10th of your e-book market sales, but can make up to a 1/3 of your income due to their higher selling price. As such, you should definitely consider them. However, realise that promotional strategies and promotional channels dedicated purely for audiobooks are still in their infancy.

Print

Here are some options within print:

- Mass market paperbacks (these are smaller in size and use cheaper quality paper. They are often only viable if produced in the thousands, but can bring the price of paperbacks down to near e-book levels).
- Paperbacks (soft cover, often done in Print-on-Demand)
- Hardcovers
- Large print versions of paperbacks & hardcovers.

Print as an indie book publisher will make up about 1% of your sales or less. This number is significantly different for traditional publishers. I've seen numbers from 20-50% of income coming from print distribution (or higher!). If you do go with a traditional publisher, they will handle the production of your print works, and as such, you won't have to worry about it as much. However, in return for accepting cost of production, as a traditional author, you receive anywhere from 6-15% of retail price (depending on format and contract) and will have to contend with return withholdings as well.

Having more options for print on your product page can *price anchor* your e-book price, making it seem cheaper. Large print is often purchased not by individuals, but libraries. If you are producing large print work, make them in hardcover as that is the preferred format for libraries. Print-on-Demand is expensive. Check out services like KDP Print & Ingram Spark.

Other Product Types

Here are some other somewhat common publishing product types. These are common in the sense that they are viable product types, but are not commonly exploited by indie publishers.

- Co-authoring works in another universe
- Licensing works in your universe to other authors
- Shared world anthologies
- Comics
- Movies/TV
- Foreign translations
- Webnovels or webseries

Making Decisions Strategically

Knowing your budget and what you can afford, consider whether you can afford to:

- Have audiobooks
- Have multiple versions of your print
- Make translations

- Make a comic and use it as a 'loss leader' for your work

If you answered no to the above questions, what licensing rights (i.e. rights to produce the products) are you keeping aside to license to third parties? What products – and quality of the product – will you accept? If you don't want to pay for foreign translations, will Babelcube work? Are you willing to accept really bad translations to be first in market? How about a comic? What product types do you envision for your world, for your marketing? Can you make bite-sized pieces of your work for audio via a podcast? Maybe you should instead write a webnovel and make your money that way and only release your work in retailers later? How about creating a short story or novella as a loss leader (a product that is given away/sold at a 'loss' to entice new customers) instead to build up your e-mail list? Or you could write a short for your dedicated fans who want to see more of the world.

Think about the products, the ways you can expand your product range, and how it fits into your *timeline* and your overall *brand and marketing strategy*. Products, as writers, don't just include the book you wrote, but all the books you can write in that universe, all the shorts, all the ways you can make the same story different – or maybe even entirely new series.

Product Type Examples			
Print	E-book/Digital Print	Audio & Visual	Miscellaneous
• Paperback • Hardcover • Large print paperback or hardcover • Mass media pocketbooks • Board books • Comic serials • Trade paperbacks • Etc.	• Webserial websites & applications (e.g. Wattpad, Royal Road, Tapas, etc.) • Epub, mobi, PDF • Personal website (blog posts, etc.) • Anthology collections • Short stories • Co-authored work extensions	• Podcasts • Audiobooks • Digital chapter files (e.g. Bandcamp) • Youtube channels • Cartoon / Anime productions • TV & Film licenses • Radio plays • Etc.	• Video games • App games • Text games • Merchandise (posters, bookmarks, scarves, mugs, etc.) • Toys (bobbleheads, stuffed toys, etc.) • Entertainment parks • Food • Etc.

The Product Life Cycle

Now that we've talked about products and the various ways you should consider how your product can be created, it's time to consider product life cycle management. The idea behind product life cycle management is that each product – in our case, we can look at it as either a book, a series or a genre – has distinct phases. The idea is that how you handle the product life cycle varies, so knowing where you are at, you can play with it.

Basically, there are three assumptions made when we look at a product life cycle:

1. Products have a limited lifespan (i.e. declining interest after a certain period)
2. Product sales pass through distinct stages, each posing different challenges, opportunities, and problems to the seller.
3. Products require different marketing, financing and time requirements at each stage.

The Four Stages of a Product Life Cycle

Introduction: This is when a book launches or is first introduced (via cover reveals, mentions on a blog, etc.). The goal of the introduction stage is to build product awareness, start people on the sales funnel, and get them excited. At this point, the fixed cost of producing your book, your time, editing, cover costs, etc. is very high. Your returns are thus in the negative for the most part.

Growth: In this stage, the product has been introduced and has some customers. The goal here is to increase the customer base, by expanding promotions, to get the product into more hands. This

> *Sidenote* – these cycles (or you might see them called 'cliffs') are not the same for all retailers, nor are they likely to stay the same for Amazon.
>
> Remember, the retailer's job at the end of the day is to sell the most number of books. Pushing new product is generally the best way, but a work that consistently sells well will still be promoted.

is where most people throw their marketing dollars, buying ads and newsletter promotions, excitedly telling everyone about the new release. If you think of the Amazon cycles (14,30,60 and 90-day algorithm cycles) this is often within the first 14 days when Amazon is really pushing and might/might not drop promotional efforts for your work.

This stage can last for a while, depending on how fast uptake of your product occurs. This can also extend for the full month (30-day cliff on Amazon).

Maturity: In the mature stage of a product, it's been out in the market for a while. A while can vary for each book and genre, from a few weeks to a few years. For us indie publishers, this could literally be between 14-28 days after you released the book. Amazon isn't pushing your book as hard anymore, so you need to get in there and do your own marketing. At this point, the vast majority of early adopters and the early majority should have picked up your product. The late majority are who you should be targeting. Furthermore, you are looking at people who have heard about your product but are still on the fence.

At this point, one thing you could possibly do is market to other audiences, putting additional people into your sales funnel to bring in new readers. This could be via other newsletters, Facebook ads, AMS ads, newsletter swaps, etc. Hopefully, you've earned back your initial outlay and returns are better. Your upfront cost as a publisher is gone, so it's just the variable cost of marketing. Many publishers/ authors start lagging at this stage, forgetting about their 'backlist'.

As mentioned, this period can be anywhere from 14 days after your release (for extremely hungry but small markets) to after the 90 day cliff (for most). In a mature product scenario, your goal is to draw in as many customers as possible for the product before it declines entirely.

Saturation & decline: This is where your book has reached the vast majority of readers in the market. No one is buying book 1 again because either they've discounted it or they've bought it. This is the 1/4 of the product adoption chart, which is shown below, where you're getting laggards in. Your market in the genre is 'filled' and for the book itself, *additional marketing to the current audience is wasting good money.*

There are two things to consider here:

- This is assuming you have not expanded your initial audience, which means, in many cases, expanding your marketing to new areas. Expanding promotion to new audiences is a way to gain new readers, which is why – at times – writing in multiple genres with multiple series can lead to sale increases in old series. This is why having *more* books out is good. It can also just be targeting new people with your Facebook ads or other promotional tactics (see above).
- This assumes you haven't or don't intend to release your next book in series yet. Realise that you can look at the stages of the lifecycle for individual products and a *series* too. At that point, the marketing for book 1 might be best achieved to catch up the laggards by releasing book 2. Or 3. Or whatever book you are looking to release.

The Production Adoption Cycle

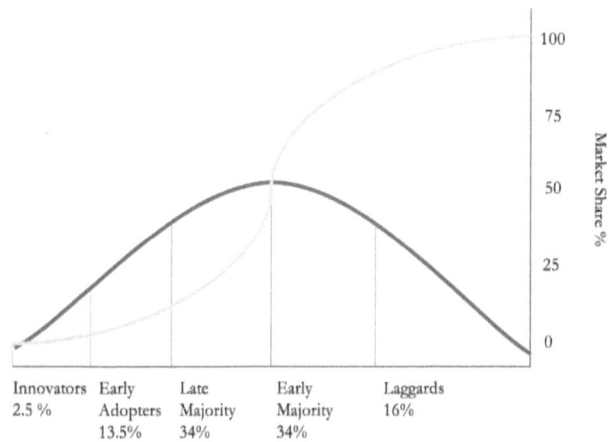

I mentioned laggards in the above section. This is a chart depicting technological adoption that has some relevance to this discussion – basically, how people pick up new innovations (or books, etc.

The yellow line is % of market saturation, blue line is the groups adopting. Something to think about if you're looking at where you are when you're marketing your product.

As It Pertains to the Publishing Industry

The biggest question to ask is – does this model work with the publishing industry/individual books or series.

The answer, in my mind, is sort of?

It can be arguable because certain works transcend basic product lifecycle management (especially public domain work). It's also arguable about whether the 'market' ever saturates per se, because new readers are always growing up and entering the market. I've read before that many markets cycle in around 5- 7 years for reading, where new readers come in and old readers fall out. And so, 'old' books which were saturated in the old market might be able to come back, restarting the life cycle in a few years.

Furthermore, as an indie publisher, if you are writing in a 'broad' genre like space opera, it's very, very unlikely that your initial book will ever reach the 'mature' stage or saturation. There are *so* many readers and your marketing budget is so tiny in comparison. Look at the sales between James Patterson for a thriller and even the highest selling indie publisher. There's a difference of millions, but if you can catch even 10%, you'd be making a pretty good living.

As with most models, take it with a grain of salt and realise it's trying to describe something complex in a few words.

Major Takeaways

- Products shift and 'grow old' for individuals
- You can saturate a market (think of a market as a marketing channel like say a Facebook group); so remember to not overstay your welcome and spread it out
- You can, often, compress the product adoption cycle using certain tactics, but there will always be early adopters and laggards. Affecting the early adopters can speed up your adoption speed. However, you will face diminishing returns on your marketing spend as you saturate a market
- Plan your timeline around the stages and how fast you want each stage to hit. Consider how introduction of your product (& series!) works, how you'll hit the growth stage and what marketing you'll use and then, how to push the product into early and late adopters (the bulk of your market) and in what timeframe

Growth Share Matrix for Writing

The Growth Share Matrix for Writing raises the concept of different points your portfolio of books might be at, how you want to view them, how you want to adjust your time and financial spend across multiple genres. When thinking about my own writing for the next year, I started by looking at the Boston Consulting Group (BCG) Matrix.

For those that don't know, this is what it looks like:

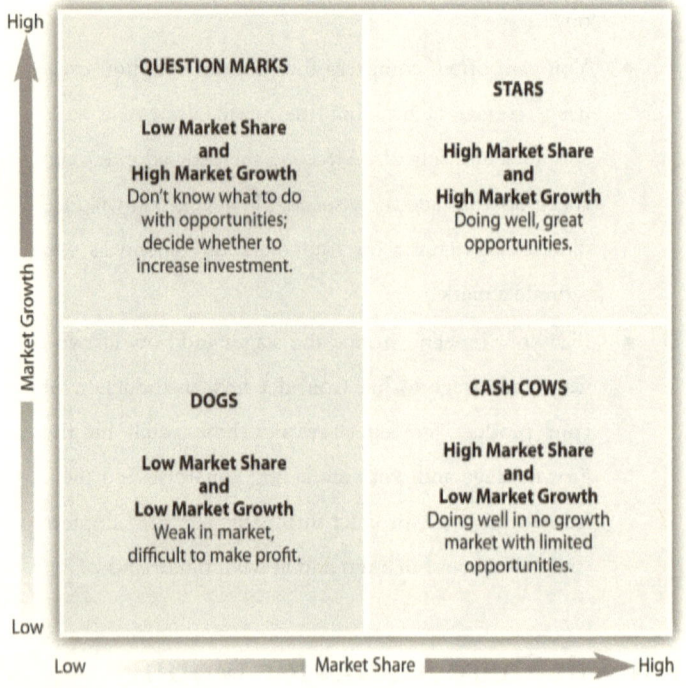

Basically, the idea is that you split your business units/brands/ what have you along those lines. It's useful if, for example; you had multiple series (like I do) where you needed to divert resources to (i.e. your writing time and working capital) and decide what to do. In my case, my Star would be A Thousand Li, the System Apocalypse is the Cash Cow, the Question Mark is Adventures on Brad and Hidden Wishes would be my dog.

Of course, that doesn't line up directly; but it does kind of give you an idea of where my resources might be worth devoting to. But…

A Series Profitability/Effort Matrix

I think there's another variation on this that could be just as, if not more useful.

In this case, I'd alter the axis to:

- Y-Axis – Series Profit
- X-Axis: Effort / Time Taken to Release each book

So, it'd be something like this:

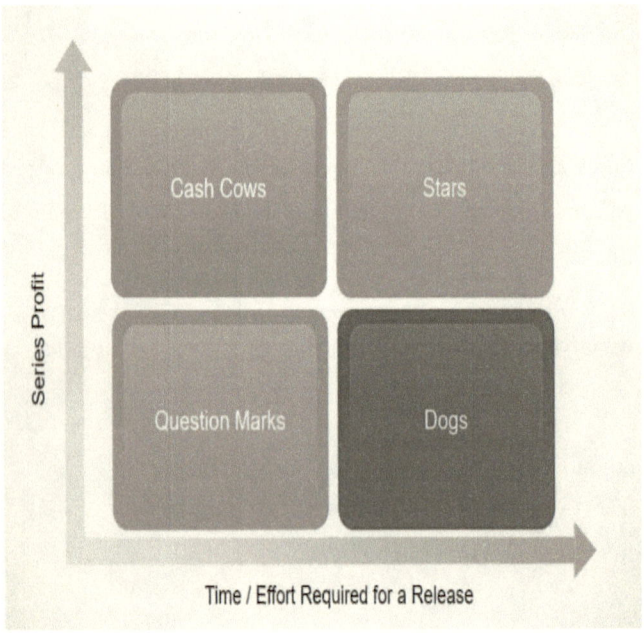

In this sense, my Series would change a little. For example:

- Cash Cow – Adventures on Brad (AoB)
- Stars – A Thousand Li & The System Apocalypse
- Dogs – Hidden Wishes
- Question Marks – translations

AoB is easy to write and at around 40k words each book, they are quick to get out. While they haven't gotten a lot of support in recent releases, I still do pull in a decent profit overall because they're now at 6 books out. Whereas Hidden Wishes at only 60k words is a pain to write. Seriously, it takes me as long to write a Hidden Wishes book as a A Thousand Li or System Apocalypse.

Just note, the use of this matrix is only useful if you have more than one (or two) series. Without those series – or potentially, product types if you write novels & shorts as an example – it is not as useful.

Some Things to Note

- There's something to be said about defining profit and what timeline you are using to define it in. As a self-pub author, you have the entirety of your career for a book to make a profit. Depending on country, it could be up to 70 years after your passing, while in other countries it could be shorter. When we decide to cut-off that timeline is a good question
- This matrix is only useful if you are like me and can 'decide' to some extent what to write. I know some writers who can only write what their muse tells them. I know others who have to finish the story they start (which, really, I recommend most people do). Again, this is another discussion; but if you don't / can't

choose what to write, making calculations of what series to write is kind of useless

- Be careful of how you define effort vs. time. For me, I am using both the amount of time it took (days/weeks/months) and how emotionally drained it made me.
- Lastly, you aren't comparing like-to-like. Series might not have the same number of books, they might not be hitting the same genre, they might have different price points. This is a 2-axis matrix, meant to help guide thinking; not dictate it.

Product Line Management

This is something to consider when you have multiple product lines (series) to play with. But I wanted to introduce another thought, which might change things around for you a little with regard to the series management, and that's the 'refreshing' or 'relaunching' approach to series.

What if you had a good product, that is in a high growth market, that for one reason or another never launched well? With the ease of updating and editing e-books, isn't it easy to relaunch? Change covers, change blurbs, take the entire thing down and then edit it maybe for a bit? And do a quick launch period, one after the other? Could you make a Question mark series a Star series? Add the fact that there's only so much work you can do per series before you have to sit back and wait a bit, and considerations like this definitely arise.

To Series or Not?

Another author consideration/indie publisher consideration is whether to do series or not. There are very, very good arguments as an indie publisher to do a series. Specifically, that every book in a **good** series pushes up sales for every book in the previous series. This is mostly due to the renewed interest and ranking of the newly released book.

As your book should be linked to previous books in the series by title and on the product page, people who see book 8 of a series then can jump back to book 1, especially if there's significant social proof (like Bestseller tags, reviews, etc.) to indicate the new release and the series is good.

It's important to consider that series do have a 'lifespan', where each book reduces in the number of readers. You can expect maybe 60-90% of readers from the first book to pick up your second book. And 80-90% of readers to read book three onwards, with each new book seeing fewer readers. And this reduction is for 'good' series. Unsuccessful series will see less than 50% of book 1 readers reading book 2.

Now, if you have a significant number of readers, that decline in the number of readers doesn't matter as much. If you have 10,000 readers for book 1, by book 5 you might have around 5,000 readers (80% book 2, 90% book 3 onwards). But if you have 1000 readers of book 1, that means you have around 500 readers for book 5. That might not be sufficient to cover your cost.

When writing series, you can also have multiple 'entry points' to a series, allowing readers to find their way in at multiple points and giving you multiple ways to promote the series. Some authors spend their entire writing careers in just one universe, writing multiple series within the universe. Others write books that are standalone but are part of the series, allowing multiple entry points that way.

I like doing series arcs, so it might be the same series but I can do longer arcs, with multiple entry points (of sorts). On the other hand, one thing about first books is that they are almost always the bestselling book in a series in terms of total units sold and revenue generated.

If you do standalone novels and have a very strong author brand or are in genres that lean towards such standalone works (horror as an example), it's possible that it might work out well for you. This, by the way, is a supposition. I don't know of my any of my indie author friends who do solely stand-alones (but I run in the scifi & fantasy circles).

Other Product Considerations – Release Speed

Lastly, one more thing to think about in terms of product considerations. This comes back to writing speed (and thus release speed), and capital to some extent. If you can write fast, you can release fast. That can kickstart your release cycle again, giving you a boost in terms of retailer algorithms and a 'natural' promotional opportunity.

In that sense, I wanted to raise one specific tactic:

Rapid release.

That is, launching one book every week/two weeks/a month until you have 3/4 books launched. Or the entire series. This kind of veers between tactic and strategy, since there are some major considerations that are strategic in nature but it's also very specific in its methodology. In either case, knowing your writing speed, knowing how fast you can backlog a bunch of books (or chapters in a serial, or audiobooks if you have money or whatever) will determine if you can use this tactic. There are definite tactical advantages to this, and the same can be said for things like backlogging chapters for Patreon, etc.

The Second P of Marketing: Pricing

Let's tackle the one we all like talking about first. Pricing. How much should you price your book at? What's the best price? It really depends on your strategy and your goals. However, there are certain external considerations you do have to consider when pricing on Amazon and other retailers (see the note on Amazon pricing model below). Below, I'm going to discuss a bunch of pricing strategies from the world of generic marketing and how it pertains to publishing. After that, we'll discuss some specific things I've learnt about pricing in publishing. Here are a few common pricing strategies from the world of marketing.

Premium Pricing

A high price, premium pricing strategy might make you look like a trad publisher. You price your books at $9.99, have great covers and try to hit up press and other (well known) traditional authors to provide blurbs and as marketing targets to help provide the air of legitimacy. This might get you fewer sales, but each of those sales are going to pay you much, much more. You'll have a smaller base of readers, but those readers are also likely to be less sensitive to the price, assuming you don't lower it later (unless for special circumstances). This can be a very slow growth strategy and in publishing, it really needs to be supported by the other 3 P's (Placement, Promotion & Product), which we'll discuss in later chapters.

Price Skimming

High price, low quality items. I'd say that Webnovel (the translated Chinese Webnovel site) is a great example of this. In Webnovel (and some other online serial sites); some chapters are provided free. At a certain point, access to additional (new) chapters must be purchased. The cost of purchasing access to a new chapter – and thus the entire book – is generally very high. The quality of the products (the novels and the translations) are often quite low, but for Webnovel in particular, they have first mover advantage and they are milking it for everything they can.

The goal with Price Skimming is to produce and distribute products as fast as you can into a hot market and when the market cools (as new entrants come in); you leave for another hot market. This is a decent strategy for write-to-trend authors who don't mind creating a million and one pen names or for webserial writers who can produce significant content on demand.

Penetration Pricing

New entrant to the market? Need to make a name for yourself? Maybe having a low, low price (normally in our world $0.99 or Free) might get you sales.

The idea behind this kind of strategy is market development. You can see some of this strategy in permafree books. This is where you are hoping to get people to read more if you give them a 'taste' of your writing. It's clearer in other areas where a new entrant to a crowded market might offer a limited time low price with very, very heavy marketing to 'steal' readers from others, or a restaurant having a few months of 'just opened' sales for their food.

One thing to consider is how big the market is. Doing this in fantasy which has millions of readers might still allow you to generate a decent income (by giving away book one, you'd drive them to pick up the remainder of your series as well as improve the rankings of your book afterwards to generate further sales when it stops being free).

But what if you are writing, for example, Fairy-tale romance? What if your total readership is in the thousands? If you are giving away book one, you might be harming your total sales since the number of readers are extremely constrained.

The other issue is ensuring you can reach these readers. A sale that no one knows of, is no more use than a non-sale. Again, know your market and tie it into your whole marketing strategy.

Cost-Plus Pricing

This is the simplest and least-applicable pricing method for indie publishers. You figure out your cost (a good thing!) and then, you work out your unit cost (impossible with e-books & PoD in general since your cost of delivery of the next book is basically $0 – yes there might be a delivery fee, but that's charged after sale) and then you add a specific markup. This is great for manufacturers. Not so useful for writers who basically have a fixed cost of production. Ignore for the most part. Other than making sure you work out your cost of production.

Competitive Pricing

This is quite simple. Look at the pricing your competitors are using. Price yourself to match.

In terms of books, you're looking at:

- Page counts/word counts
- Equivalent level of covers & blurbs

- Preferably equivalent level of fame (or fame that you want to reach)
- Product quality.

If you want to be or think you are a market leader in writing and want to be like them, you price to match their prices. By being priced the same as the market leaders, you signal you're as good as they are. If the rest of your product isn't…well, you've got a problem. But it can also mean that new people in the market might be 'tricked' into assuming you're as important, and thus be willing to buy your work at the higher price. At worst, you've basically taken away one negative. No one's thinking about 'can I afford to buy this specific book' if your product is the same price as every other product out there. The rest of your P's come into play now.

Price Discrimination

Do you price differently for different geographic markets? If so, you're doing price discrimination (geographic). You can also do it (to some extent) with regard to retailers (since Amazon doesn't promise to price match anymore). If you don't think you do it yet, if you have audiobooks, e-books & print, you probably are doing price discrimination.

But there are other ways of doing price discrimination beyond retailer, geographic and product formats. You can price discriminate by time (see below), series order (cheaper first in series, most expensive last in series, etc.), word count, genre, bundles or distribution type (Kindle Unlimited, your retail store, etc.) as a few examples.

End of the day, price discrimination requires you to be able to segment your target markets such that it is more difficult for those who you discriminate against to pick up the other product and/or the product itself is different (e.g. audiobook, e-book, print, etc.).

Unlike many other retailers, a lot of price discrimination options are removed from you if you work only through retailers. If you have your own webstore, you can further refine price discrimination using coupon codes and the like. Otherwise, you are (to some extent); dependent on the retailers.

Time-Based Pricing

You see this kind of pricing strategy with computers and other products that deteriorate over time (bread, meat, etc.). Early adopters are charged a premium price, with price dropping as quality/demand drops. You see this in high prices for pre-orders and then, later on, a slow lowering of prices in some older 'backlist' books. Or increased 'promo pricing' for these books. It is more common to have time-based pricing happen in combination with 'bundle' pricing, where multiple books are added and then the entire price is lowered.

Captive Product Pricing

Last book in the series? Got a big finale? Raise the price. Milk those readers for every penny they're worth. After 9/12/20 books, they're most likely going to buy that last book just to read it. Otherwise, you might have other secondary series that have to be read to understand what is going on (Marvel Comic crossovers anyone?), forcing people to buy more. It's a valid strategy, if annoying as a consumer.

Promotional Pricing

Promotional pricing is when you lower the regular price to make your product more attractive to a larger market of cost-conscious consumers. Used effectively, promotional pricing can create a larger pool of readers to pull down your sales funnel.

But be careful. Cost conscious customers who only buy at $0.99 might balk at being asked to buy your next books at $4.99 or $5.99, which means you might have to (eventually) discount your later books. Timing on promotional pricing is important, but it can be very useful for generating significantly more revenue. Part of it is because (on Amazon), you are pushed up higher on their search results when you are selling more, so an increase in sales can offer some help in their search and display algorithms. This is true for all retailers too to greater – Google Play – or lesser – Kobo – degrees.

Side note – Amazon is doing more discounting on 1-day sales surges and looking at trends, so having more regular or widespread promotional pushes over a longer period of time is more likely to push your ranking up and keep you high in the ranks.

Bundle Pricing

Got more than 1 book? Bundle pricing is what happens when you slide multiple books into one deal. The most common is creating omnibus editions (like my Adventures on Brad Books 1-3) but you can also see it in other areas, if you have control. For example, in-convention sales where you sell 3 sets of your paperbacks for $40 instead of $45. Or on your personal direct sales website (like my Payhip store) and offer say, a purchase of a short story at $0.99 if they buy the main books in the series already.

In terms of book publishing, the big things to think about are:

- Timing of when to release am omnibus

- Audiobook hours (getting over that 15 hour total makes sales on Audible increase significantly among credit users as it now over the $1/listening hour threshold!)
- Selective promotion of the omnibus and the read-through for on-going books.

There are tactics to use with bundled items, but we're talking strategy. I'm just going to say that it's an option and something to slide into your marketing plan when you are building it.

Anchor Pricing

Anchor pricing is the use of a (generally higher) price to set up a benchmark in the mind of the consumer. You then have a lower price that makes your product a deal. You see this with sale prices displayed next to the regular price in supermarkets and other retailers. For us indie publishers – having a paperback priced at $15 will allow Amazon (and other retailers) to favorably compare it to your e-book price (of $3-6). This is useful, because it increases conversion rates of purchases and also allows you to command a higher price.

Here's the hidden danger. If you saw a product normally priced at $16 and is now priced at $1, would you buy it? Or are you asking *why* first? If that product was say, fish, would you pause and think, 'is that fish fresh?' Be careful about using anchor pricing and pricing your e-book too low on a *regular basis*. You don't want people thinking your product is 'bad fish'.

Kindle Unlimited (KU)

This is the giant boogeyman. To have your book available in the Kindle Unlimited program (seen as the Kindle Lending Program in your dashboard), you have to have your e-book distributed exclusive with Amazon. In return, your product is the equivalent of $0 for subscribers. While it's not free for subscribers to part of the program, your *individual* book is.

This actually creates a Price Discriminatory pricing strategy – $4.99 for non-KU subscribers, $0 for KU subscribers. Since authors can subscribe for periods of 3 months into the Kindle Lending Program, you can make this a time-based promotion (by emphasising that your books will be removed after 3 months, etc.).

In addition, by being part of the KU program, you have the advantage of dropping your price further; to $0.99 or Free with their promotional options. It opens a ton of tactical options over the year, since it's time limited and requires significantly less adjustments than normal. However, there are drawbacks to being exclusive to only Kindle Unlimited that will be discussed under distribution strategy later in the book.

KU enrollment has multiple effects on the entire marketing strategy and can't really be considered by itself. Just realise that it is quite, quite useful and important in some genres. The siren call of 'free' is very, very attractive to readers.

Making Pricing Decisions as an Indie Publisher

One of the biggest issues I have with indie publishers is that they sell themselves short. All the damn time. They price themselves too low – taking the minimum amount at $2.99 to make something. Forgetting that they can earn a lot more with fewer people. Often, I hear people say 'but I'm not that good' or 'I don't want people to pay that much for this'.

It's often an issue of confidence – in themselves, in their work – rather than an actual business decision. At the end of the day, how much people pay is up to them.

On top of that, so many authors price low and end up driving the entire market low. If you don't believe me, watch some of the romance markets. So many books are sold at $0.99. And the reason they have to do it is because everyone else does it. How much more could they earn if people kept their pricing at $2.99? Who knows? Maybe they are right. Because of how many whale readers (large scale readers) there are, maybe it's not viable to have

$0.99 at all without significant quick price changes. But…I'm leery of prices going down because I've seen how destructive it is in my old business. Remember, as a writer, in many ways, your product is unique. Or it should be in most cases, if you aren't chasing trends and switching pen names. But that's another discussion.

As indie publishers, one of the biggest advantages we have in pricing is the ability to experiment, test, and get our results back fast. Is $4.99 the right price? Or $3.99? Should I do a combination of $4.99 with $0.99 promos every 3 months? Or every 6 months? How about pricing your book 1 at $0.99 permanently but having every other book at $5.99? Or less extreme at $4.99 and $5.99?

Is it worth it?

Who knows? Your books are different than mine, your marketing strategy, your product base is all different. But guess what? You can test it out and find out. Yes, sometimes, it takes a few months to work out results. But you can test and keep testing. And if you have multiple product lines (read series!); you can test on one or two and never affect your main sellers. So, test.

The Third P of Marketing: Placement

Place or distribution as it may be is the question of how you're going to get your product to your target market. The methods and the locations, not in what form. We have dealt with questions like whether to make audiobooks or print mass market paperbacks already. Now, you're asking the question on how best to make sure it arrives in locations where your audience is. And that's the critical part of the marketing strategy for distribution. Making sure the distribution choices you make fit those of your audience.

An example of great distribution strategy is Scholastic, a multinational company which produces and distributes children's books and educational materials. Their promotion and distribution through schools and direct to kids ensures that they have a stranglehold of the market. Sure, they could distribute their books at new stands or mass-market retailers, but the best way? Via schoolrooms where the kids are able to see their friends get things and they themselves can order what they want direct.

Your Target Market

As mentioned, when looking at distribution strategy, one of the things you have to consider is where your target market is located. This goes back to understanding your target market, understanding how they shop and their preferences in shopping.

The other consideration, and this comes into play with the SWOT & PEST analysis you've done, is where your competitors are already doing business. At times, this can be a great indicator of locations that you should target because that's where the audience is congregating.

At other times, this could indicate locations you might want to avoid because you want to tap into untouched markets with your books. A great example of this could be in my own genre (LitRPG) where the vast majority of the market is in Kindle Unlimited. There's an argument then that instead of joining the throngs fighting for market share in Kindle Unlimited, you should focus on the wide market to gain sales. While there might be a smaller (current) audience, you'd be able to gain a much larger share of that audience and grow the market yourself.

The Breakdown

Now, I'm going to split the distribution considerations into basically three major options, just to simplify matters. These are:

- Exclusive (often Amazon exclusive)
- Wide (that is, distribute as widely as possible via as many retailers)
- Direct sales

Now, there are other options and tactical level details on this, but I want to back off for a second and point out that the vast, vast majority of independent publishers make the majority of their income from digital sales. Some might make anywhere from a third to half via audiobooks and the other two thirds via e-book (or e-book equivalent) sales. But print is very, very rarely more than 1 or 2%.

For the majority of individuals, due to capital, expertise and time limitations, it's electronic distribution that is important. Still, it's worthwhile understanding print distribution as a whole to understand one's options.

A Brief Note on Print Distribution

There are two major forms of print creation: print-on-demand (PoD) and offset printing (mass printing).

Print-on-Demand

Print-on-demand is what the significant majority of independent publishers use - if they even bother to create paperback copies of their work. Remember, print is often only 1% of the total sales revenue of most indie publishers (sometimes as low as 0.01%!). The individuals not using print-on-demand in an indie publishing setting can often be individually named. That's how rare not using PoD is.

Now, print distribution can be done directly on Amazon or via PoD companies like Ingram Spark or Lulu.

Print distribution via PoD is often 'wide' and allows you access to independent book retailers and libraries. With a company like Ingram Spark, you can even offer substantial discount and returns as an option for your print distribution, making it more likely that independent bookstores will stock and keep your books on their shelves as they can return the books for zero cost (to them). You, however, will be charged the cost of production and shipping cost of the books returned. This can result in a negative balance if your books do not sell.

While it is often a low revenue stream of income for most indie publishers, having PoD books does mean that you open up new distribution, promotion and sales options (like signed copies and giveaways) that are unavailable to those who do not have paperbacks.

In general, if you do decide to create a PoD paperback, you should distribute as widely as possible through as many distributors as it makes sense to increase the chance of sales in distribution locations (independent retailers and libraries) and geographic regions. This will, eventually, increase reach and sales for you. The best way to do this is to use Amazon and print distribution companies who have printing facilities in countries outside of North America.

Offset/Mass Printing

This is an area I am less directly knowledgeable about. It is possible to hire and pay for offset printing of your work directly. In most cases, offset printing will require an order of hundreds if not thousands of books. With offset printing, the greater the number of copies printed in a single print run, the lower the per unit cost. This is why mass market paperbacks by traditional publishers can be sold at $7-8 a book, due to the cost of printing being significantly lower as they are producing tens of thousands of such books.

The most common method I know of to do offset printing on a mass volume method is to do a Kickstarter, generating sales beforehand for a portion of the printed copies. Then, the remaining printed copies are sent to a storage location.

From there, the author has two options for mass distribution - directly contacting and selling books to retailers (indie bookstores and the like) or contacting a book distribution company which specialises in promoting and selling paperback books to indie retailers.

This is a very risky distribution/product method due to the high capital cost involved, and is, as mentioned, rarely done by indie authors. The few that I know who do this are highly sophisticated marketers who have built a strong brand name. Independent retailers and mass-market retail chains rarely touch indie books (partly due to cost and lack of ability to do returns, and partly due to low sell-through), so you have to be willing to market and push sales.

It's worth remembering that bookstores at the end of day care about sell-through (the volume of sales of a specific product — that is, how often it is sold out) more than anything else. If you can stock your book in a store and it sells through constantly, they will stock your work. However, to get that consistent sell-through, your book needs to attract their customer base (i.e. walk-in customers); or you have to be able to send your regular customers to them.

Of course, to get your initial book into the store itself is a significant impediment. Individuals who have managed this have often cited being local and making in-person appearances at the store. Even then, it should be noted that this is a difficult distribution method to make work.

Again, this is a risky strategy and one I personally have no experience with and only have the related examples of other authors to go from. It's something to do more research into if you have a significant author brand and capital.

Last note, I wrote the above with the eye of one going in as an indie publisher. If you do decide to sign with a traditional publisher with deep ties into the retail side of the industry, concerns about capital cost of print production, the distribution and storage of your books and (to some extent) the marketing of said books will be reduced significantly. Of course, you might also not see much in terms of royalties, but that's part of the usual deal with trad publishing.

The Exclusive Option

You'll see this discussion a lot in author groups discussing going exclusive (or KDP Select, more commonly called Kindle Unlimited due to that being the front-end term) or going wide - meaning, using many other distributors. The reason this discussion appears as often as it does is due to the restrictive policies Amazon has.

The two major exclusivity options at this time are:
- Kindle Unlimited for e-books
- ACX distribution for audiobooks

KDP Select (Kindle Unlimited)

Under the KDP Select exclusivity program, authors sign their books up for a period of 90 days. During that time, the books are enrolled in Kindle Unlimited which is an 'all you can read' subscription program. Readers are charged a fixed amount and have access to all books enrolled in the KDP program.

Once a month, Amazon announces the KDP Select Fund (a specific amount of money that is the 'pot') from which authors are paid. Payments are calculated based off what is known as Kindle Edition Normalised Page Counts (KENP) which are a calculated number of pages for each book (generally somewhere in the 250-350 words per page depending on formatting).

As such, each book has a 'fixed' KENP. Each page that is read by a Kindle Unlimited (KU) subscriber of your book is logged. You are then paid based off each page read with the amount paid per page varying and calculated based off how much the KDP Select Fund is that month. As such, you never have a known amount you'd earn per page as it'll vary each month.

Now, things to note:

- The per page rate is calculated for each marketplace that KU is available. As such, while the total global fund is given, that is further broken into per market fund amounts. A page read in Germany is worth less than a page read in the USA.
- The rate varies between $0.004 to $0.0048 per KENP.
- You are only ever paid for the first readthrough. Subsequent readthroughs do not pay you.
- Books can be downloaded from the KU program and kept on devices, so you can be paid months after you remove them (readers can have up to 10 books downloaded from the program).
- KDP Select pays multiple bonuses for the top 100 most page reads for a single book in the US & UK and their 'All Star' for most page reads by an author. The

requirements are roughly 2+ million page reads (in a month) for a single book or 8+ million total page reads for an account.

KU exclusivity is quite popular among certain whale reading genres. As I understand it, Science Fiction, Romance and Harem/Reverse Harem do really well, while other genres are better off wide.

A good way to ascertain how prevalent Kindle Unlimited is in your genre is reviewing the top 100 books in your genre for sales. Go to the category pages and review how many of those books are in Kindle Unlimited and how many are not. Of those, how many KU books are in the top 10. If you keep an eye on this number for a month or two, you'll have an understanding of how prevalent KU is to your specific niche.

Pros & Cons

In general, KU provides a significant boost in terms of number of books read and reduces the barriers to purchase as each KU book is basically 'free' for the reader. This allows readers (especially whale readers) to pick up and try multiple books a month.

However, KU generally depresses the price of books unless you are an epic fantasy writer or the like (where books are 300k words long). This is because while sale prices are lower, KU pays per page read, and with really long books, can earn a writer more.

This then offers the distribution & pricing strategy of low sale pricing (to help rank the book well and expose it on Amazon searches and 'also boughts' further) while being in KU. The goal then is to make money back on the KU reads.

This is somewhat reliant on the way Amazon designs their product pages where the Kindle Unlimited 'borrow' function is featured prominently rather than the 'buy' option. As such, even if you price at $0.99 (and promote it as such); for KU readers, it's easier to 'borrow' the book.

The major disadvantage (beyond potential devaluation) is the restriction in distribution locations. As an indie publisher, you become entirely reliant on Amazon for your e-book income. You *cannot* have your book on any other retailer.

ACX Exclusivity

Firstly, let's clarify ACX (Audiobook Creation Exchange) is a distribution platform for audiobooks. ACX is owned by Amazon and currently distributes to Audible (which is again, owned by Amazon) and iTunes. They do not distribute anywhere else.

ACX offers an exclusivity option which is differentiated by differing royalty rates.

- Exclusive audiobooks receive 40% royalties
- Non-exclusive audiobooks receive 25% royalties

In either case, when you sign up with ACX, you sign up for a minimum 7-year distribution agreement. If you pay for your audiobooks direct (and thus own the copyright fully instead of doing a royalty share option), you can go non-exclusive after 1 year. If not, you have to be exclusive with Audible for the full 7 years.

Pros & Cons

Now, it's worth noting that while Audible itself has anything from 27-40% or so of the audiobook market, much of that market domination is in the US & UK. As such, while the 15% that you lose by going non-exclusive can potentially be made up by going wide, Audible is a significant market and can be a very high percentage of the market for certain genres.

Secondly, ACX as you might have noted do not distribute to libraries. With the multiple distribution methods to libraries, these markets can make up a significant percentage of the income you gain when you go wide. Furthermore, touching and working with libraries can offer additional revenue streams and publicity (author talks, etc.).

Lastly, it's worth noting that in terms of promotional opportunities, the audiobook market is very limited at this time. As such, much of the growth is often on an organic (word of mouth and on-page sales promotions) basis rather than via paid promotions.

Going Wide

When indie authors talk about being 'wide', they mean not being exclusive to Amazon. This is, unfortunately, due to Amazon's predominance as a marketplace in the US & many Western European countries.

The Wide strategy predicates upon a few ideas:

- Firstly, while Amazon is the 300lb gorilla in the US and many Western European countries, its dominance is significantly less outside of those markets. Google Play, iBooks, Scribd, Kobo, etc. can often contain a higher percentage of a local market than Amazon or at least, be a significant percentage. For example, in Canada, Amazon is just 57% of the market with Kobo taking up another 25%.

- Even in the US, Amazon is only 83% of the market share *(authorearnings.com report for 2018)*. That leaves another 17% of the market that you are missing out by being exclusive.
- When the vast majority of indie authors are moving to Amazon, it leaves a dearth of books for readers in the other marketplaces. As such, you could easily become a big fish in a small pond.
- Income from a variety of sources is more stable than reliance on a single source. This is for both long-term stability (what if Amazon crashes, blocks your author account, has payment issues, etc.) and for short-term stability (sales on wide platforms are often more stable due to lower competition levels and differing algorithms, launches can and have been ruined due to technical issues – e.g. pre-orders being cancelled – or other factors outside of an author's control. The greater the number of retailers, the lower the chance).
- By being non-exclusive to Amazon, you open up the potentially lucrative library market. Library readers can often be a large source of income and new readers.
- By being wide and establishing yourself across multiple regions and retailers, you increase the chance that your particular work is a 'hit' in that specific market. A book that doesn't sell well in America might do well in India or South East Asia.

- Being wide allows you to sell direct which is (often) the highest percentage return on royalties you can get. Also, owning your own store provides you the highest amount of data for analysis and opens up tactical marketing options that might not be available otherwise (e.g. Google Adwords and conversion tracking on store)
- New product formatting options and distribution methods are open to you while you are wide. This includes subscription sales (like with Scribd) or pay per chapter programs (like with Radish and Tapas) or Patreon 'advanced chapter' options combined with web serial publishing.
- Lastly, by being wide and selling in a variety of platforms, reaching the largest number of readers as possible, you increase the chance that your work might be picked up by foreign publishers for translations.

While some of these justifications I have seen for myself (stabler income, less reliance on Amazon, more opportunities to reach new markets, library sales, product formatting and distribution options), I believe that others like foreign translation opportunities are much less likely unless you have significant sales already.

Options for Distributing Wide

Very briefly, when distributing wide, your options include direct distribution wide (i.e. signing up directly with multiple e-book retailers like Kobo, Apple, Barnes & Noble and Google Play) or going through a distributor like Smashwords or Draft2Digital (for e-books) or FindAwayVoices or Authors Republic (for audiobooks). Going through a distributor reduces your income as they take a percentage cut from your sales. The advantage though is that it's a lot easier and reduces the complexity.

The general advice is to go direct with the major market retailers (named above) to reduce the percentage taken from distributors as well as to access certain, direct only, promotional opportunities (Kobo in particular is known for this). For smaller retailers or those that do not have convenient methods to access, use D2D or the other distributors. ***In general, with a wide strategy, the best option is to distribute as widely as possible.*** That means using as many options as you can.

One other advantage of using distributors is that they often disregard minimum $ payout amounts. So, if you are selling very low in specific retailers, you will still be paid out by the distributors rather than having to wait multiple months to hit your minimum threshold if you went direct.

Direct Sales

There are a number of potential sales options where you (the author) directly interact with the public and attempt to sell your work.

Examples of such distribution options include:
- Talks or seminars you are able to sell your works
- Farmers markets/flea markets/conventions where you have paid for a space
- Your website and/or 3rd party websites that allow you to host your products (often for a fee)

The main things that differentiate direct sales from other wide retailer options in my mind are that direct sales are often limited in their reach. This limit could be due to time (conventions, flea markets, talks, etc.) or via the need to attract the audience to the selling location (i.e. your website, etc.).

Advantages and Limitations

The advantage of direct sales as a medium of distribution is that your gross profit is the highest of any other method. You often are only paying minimal fees (processing fees in most cases) for each transaction. This can amount to 5-15% depending on what system you are using. As with the same calculus of balancing indie vs trad publishing, the higher the percentage you are able to earn, the fewer copies you have to sell.

The largest limitation of direct sales is the limited audience sizes.

With conventions, talks and flea markets (i.e. in-person sales); the hope is that the organisers have developed the event sufficiently to draw in the audience for you. You are then limited to whatever audience is there (and thus must have researched the event sufficiently to make sure the target market meets *your* market). However, no matter what, your potential sales is limited to that audience and to those individuals.

On the other hand, in-person sales offers the advantage of helping to brand and create a closer connection to those you sell to directly.

With direct sales online, instead of a 3rd party organiser drawing in the audience, you will have to do so. As such, the cost of audience acquisition lands on you directly. Whether it's via Search Engine Marketing, paid advertising, social media promotions or the like, you'll have to draw in the audience.

Lastly, in both cases, such distribution efforts do require a significant investment of time. And, as always, as an author, a large part of your future income will come from the works you produce.

The Fourth P of Marketing: Promotion

Marketing promotion is a **HUGE** area. There are actual advertising agencies that focus on a single area of promotion. Covering everything in a single book or post or series of posts is impossible. Instead, I'm going to play with some basic overall concepts for people to consider. Firstly, let's talk about 'The Line' in Promotions.

Above the Line Promotions

Above the Line Promotional concepts are strategies and tactics that target large masses of people, often on only mildly differentiated levels. The biggest advantage of above the line promotions is the ability to reach a mass audience in (a per audience member reached level) cheaper rate. However, because you are touching masses, it is often more expensive (in totality!) than below the line methods.

In addition, because you are reaching large numbers, tracking results is often very difficult; and focused on things like reach, brand awareness and brand perception. Above the Line promotional strategies include TV advertising, newspaper advertising, radio ads and billboards.

Below the Line Promotions

These are Promotional tactics and strategies that focus on a smaller target market and don't focus on the 'major' advertising methods above. Often, below the line promotions are much more focused and easier to track results from. These include things like public relations, search engine marketing, social media marketing, in-person sales, events, and direct mail.

Now, if you're reading that list, you're likely realising that for **most** indie authors, below the line promotional strategies are the most affordable. And that's fine. The vast, vast majority of the time, unless you're writing in a genre that is read by a large and far reaching demographic (romance, self-help, thrillers and mysteries, we're looking at you); the chances are, above the line promotions won't work.

That being said, there are ways to be very, very specific about your marketing. For example – could you put up an advertisement on a billboard outside of a cinema when Ready Player One was out if you wrote LitRPG? It might be expensive, but that's very good targeting right there for the few weeks the movie is out.

You can also get quite a bit of radio advertising done, quite inexpensively, if you are willing to do a run of station advertisements. For information on ways to get cheap mass marketing options, check out Guerilla Marketing by Jay Conrad Levinson. Still, for the vast majority of us, what we're going to focus upon is promotions below the line.

Before we do that though, we have to talk about some concepts you need.

Sales Funnel

When you're building out your promotional strategy, make sure to consider where along the sales funnel you're reaching people and what the goal of your

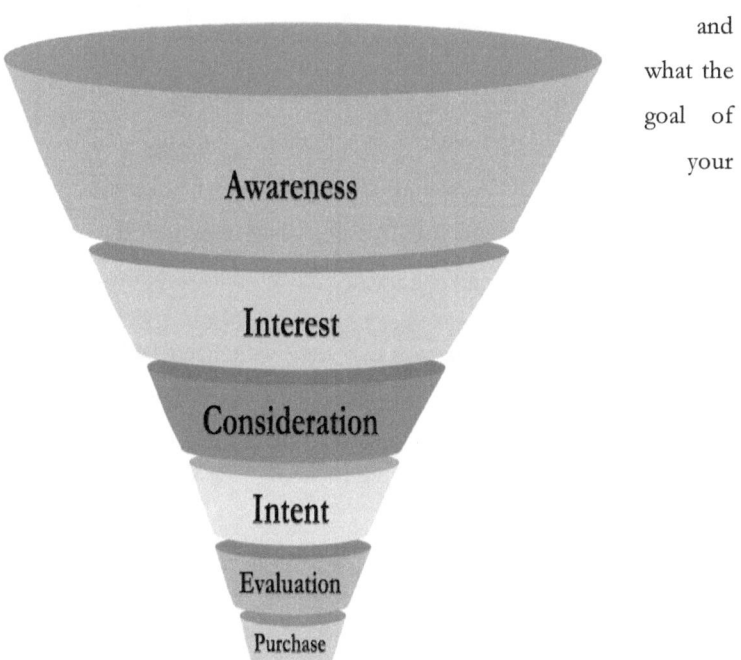

promotion is. The typical sales funnel includes the following stages: awareness, interest, consideration, intent, evaluation, and purchase:

Some promotional tactics (above the line stuff) are much, much better at doing brand awareness. Heck, even some kinds of below the line advertising (promotional posts, banner ads on websites) are more geared towards the brand awareness side than actual sales click-through.

The 10% Rule

Now that you've worked out a budget, I'd like to introduce you to what I call my 10% rule. Take your budget (marketing, production, whatever). Split off 10% of it. That's now your 'fun project' budget.

Why? The basic idea is that the vast majority of your budget should be spent on doing the things you know work. For indie writers, that's mostly producing e-books with good covers and good editing.

But, if you stick to doing only what you know will work, you never innovate. You never test.

So. 10%.

Understanding your Customers

Hopefully, you've already done this part up in the SWOT analysis. Knowing your customers (or potential customers) is key to promotions, but it's also key to understanding your business.

When you're looking at building out your understanding of customers, there are a few things you can do:

- Use tried and tested demographic information (age, sex, education, spoken languages, relationship status, jobs and job responsibilities, etc.)
- Understand key customer interest information (interests, TV series they watch, books they read, music they listen to, etc.)
- Build out buyer personas (think of how you'd describe the various customer segments that you have)
- Media consumption methods

Knowing this will let you narrow down your customers and promotional methods.

Tao Wong

The Rule of 7

That is, the Rule of 7 (or 20 or 5) for ads. Specifically, this is the idea that you need multiple interactions or views with an advertisement or brand before an individual will take action.

I put the other numbers in brackets because the research for many of those numbers is not very robust at all. That number often changes depending on the research article you read, so take any specific criteria as a 'best guess'. The idea is that you need repetition to break-through the noise that an individual experiences. Some research studies show that individuals are exposed to hundreds of brands within a few hours of waking.

The first instance of this rule came back in the 18th century by Thomas Smith. This is the full quote:

> *The first time people look at any given ad, they don't even see it.*
> *The second time, they don't notice it.*
> *The third time, they are aware that it is there.*
> *The fourth time, they have a fleeting sense that they've seen it somewhere before.*
> *The fifth time, they actually read the ad.*
> *The sixth time they thumb their nose at it.*
> *The seventh time, they start to get a little irritated with it.*
> *The eighth time, they start to think, "Here's that confounded ad again."*
> *The ninth time, they start to wonder if they're missing out on something.*
> *The tenth time, they ask their friends and neighbors if they've tried it.*
> *The eleventh time, they wonder how the company is paying for all these ads.*
> *The twelfth time, they start to think that it must be a good product.*

The thirteenth time, they start to feel the product has value.
The fourteenth time, they start to remember wanting a product exactly like this for a long time.
The fifteenth time, they start to yearn for it because they can't afford to buy it.
The sixteenth time, they accept the fact that they will buy it sometime in the future.
The seventeenth time, they make a note to buy the product.
The eighteenth time, they curse their poverty for not allowing them to buy this terrific product.
The nineteenth time, they count their money very carefully.
The twentieth time prospects see the ad, they buy what is offering.

Since then, we've had other people come up with various numbers. But how true is it?

You are not the Market

As usual, I've seen a lot of comments about how 'they buy things immediately or not at all' or 'I've never bought anything from an advertisement'. Setting aside the significant amount of research that shows **people do not know what they are doing,** it's worth remembering – you are not the market.

It's why Paco Underhill spent hours and hours watching security camera recordings of how people moved through a store. It's why Usability Designers do eye-tracking studies.

When you're marketing, put aside your own prejudice and conceptions of what *you'd do*. Look at the data and research.

Real World Experience

That being said, didn't I just say that I couldn't find research showing the number of repetitions required? Yes, but research has shown that you need repeated repetitions to increase everything from sales to brand recognition. I'm not going to dig through the numerous marketing studies to find the information, instead, I'll just tell 2 stories.

Firstly, in the early 2000's a major financial organisation was running advertisements in print papers. Specifically, they were running a couple of full page and half-page advertisements, for the usual brand awareness reasons. A smart marketer decided, instead of running a couple of large ads, they would test something out. They took their advertising budget, and without making it smaller, worked with the newspaper to create multiple smaller advertisements. These advertisements were split into sections across the entirety of the paper, from the news to entertainment sections to classifieds. Instead of two or three ads, they now had 10 or 12 (or more. I don't actually recall if they ever gave the number).

Guess what? Brand awareness and recognition shot up by a significant number after they started doing this. Significantly enough that the organisation actually won the Canadian marketing award for the year.

The story struck me, because a short time before that, I was running a test of my own.

We'd created a new website for a product I was selling. We hadn't done any marketing or advertising, so it had almost no visits and definitely no sales. We then ran an advertisement (print ad, half-page) in a single magazine. That's it. One advertisement in one magazine. It came out once a month, we booked for three months at that time. All to test the efficacy of that specific magazine.

Here's the interesting thing. First month? $350 in sales. Month 2 – $500 in sales. Month 3 – $1200 in sales.

What changed? Nothing. We still received almost no organic website visits. We had no search engine equity or rankings. The only thing that promoted the site was that single advertisement in that single magazine. Repeating, three times.

Now, there's an argument that people couldn't afford what we sold (it was a bit expensive) and so had to wait for the first few months to get their money. And that might be true. But... I have a feeling it's more the constant repetitions.

The Takeaway

Consistency and repetition of your brand is important. When building a promotional campaign, build out for the long-term with multiple touchpoints. You need to do so, to push people down the sales funnel.

A single campaign 'burst' might see quick results, but a long-term campaign will see bigger results in general. You have to keep touching your demographic, making them aware of you before they'll act. This should influence what you intend to buy, because some markets (see print newspaper ads) are too expensive to do on the regular.

Promotional Calendar

Lastly, I want you to build out a promotional calendar. Grab all your books (or series) and set them down one side. Then, across the top of the calendar columns, the months. Now, you can start inputting the various methods that you're going to use for the various series.

Things you want to consider when building a promotional calendar are:
- The danger of overlapping promotions. For example, if you have three series, promoting all three in the same

month will be expensive, create a huge spike in sales (hopefully) and mess up benchmarks.

If you are promoting all three series, there is no way to tell if you are gaining fans who might be reading over into other series, rather than just stopping at your first series.

- On-going and 'blast' promotions. For example, Amazon Marketing Services (AMS) ads are pretty much on-going promotional methods. You turn them on, you tweak for optimisation, but you shouldn't be turning them off if you're doing well (especially for book 1's). On the other hand, newsletter promo sites are often 'blast' promos. The e-mail newsletter goes out, sales spike, but you don't have another promo continuing at the same time.

- Coinciding promo sales with promo periods. This is pretty basic, but if you have only 5 days for 'cheap' or promo sales (e.g. if you are in KU); you need to know when those are when you get them 'refreshed'. Not knowing that can cause problems.

- New release months and promos set-up for those release months. Maybe you have book 4 coming out of your on-going series. If that's the case, having a promo of book 1 a few days before or during the release of book 4 might make sense to drum up interest and/or drive sales to your books by working with the rank increase.

- Benchmark months (i.e. months where no new promotional opportunities or sales are occurring) are important too. Just because you can run promos all the time, doesn't mean you should. It can be just as useful and important to have a few 'quiet' months, so that you can benchmark what your new 'base' of sales are. This is important as well if you've started turning on a lot of on-going promotions and know they are doing okay, but aren't sure what your 'base' sales are without blast promotions, without releases, etc. Having a few quiet months can give you that period, where you can tell that your new 'base' is $2,000 on that $300 ad spend.

- Seasonal/annual bias and other events. You might want to consider how certain periods can affect your sales. Certain books sell better during the summer periods, others in winter. You can also check against the promos that trad publishers do (often they gear up towards the fall/winter season, so it might be better to avoid it depending on your genre); etc. Heck, even your competitors in the niche might be important. If there's a single dominant author, you might want to avoid releasing when they do.

- Lastly, you'll want to consider cashflow when creating your promos. If you have low or high sales months (i.e.

release months), you might want to consider how that'll affect your ability to pay for your promotions as well as what you can do to bolster low sales months up (and generate a more consistent flow of revenue). That is, if you want or care about that.

By the way, along with the promotional calendar, I also use a simple Google Calendar that is much more specific about changes. I might put on the Google Calendar the date I put something on pre-order, the date I change a blurb, the date I switched up my ad copy or when I started A/B testing multiple ads. Having both a general calendar and specific calendars are important, especially when you start looking 3/4 years in the future.

The Basic Promotional Toolbox

We've now covered the theoretical concepts of marketing promotions the tools that you need to have a proper promotional strategy, and what you need to consider when building out your promotional calendar. Now, let's discuss the 'basic' building blocks which I think should be the core part of any promotional toolbox.

Author Website

Firstly, you need a place where your readers can find you and, just as importantly, find information about your next book and their release dates.

Read that again.

That is the most important information your readers are looking for when they come to your website. You need to let them know when book 2/3/4/etc. is going to be released and when/where they can buy those books. Everything else is superfluous unless you are trying to make yourself the brand. In that case, then, yes, your website will need to have your branding content on it (pictures of your kittens, the food you cook, daily musings, etc.). For most though, you'll need a contact page, a series page with links to where to buy your book, and new release information. That's it.

I use WordPress myself, along with a bunch of plugins. You can add things like Google Analytics and the Facebook Pixel as well as Amazon Associate accounts to your website to add information. They are all useful, but not necessary. A contact page, a series page, and new release information? Necessary.

Lastly, a website is a great place for you to start converting browsers looking for information into newsletter subscribers.

There are numerous ways to integrate website forms, and most of them are really simple.

A Newsletter

Next up, you need a newsletter. I'm going to recommend that you use one of the newsletter systems out there – like Sendfox, Mailerlite, etc. This is because they are set-up to handle mass e-mailing and to deal with the privacy and other legal concerns about e-mailing people (e.g. did you know that you need to have an address on your newsletters that people can send mail to? Yes, really.).

I generally recommend that you create 2 mailing lists. The first is the organic mailing list, those people who subscribe to your newsletter off the back of your books, off your website or Facebook integration. The second mailing list comes from use of other mailing list sites like Story Origin or Bookfunnel. You'll have to build that list slowly, and generally, you'll have to build it via giving away free books, chapters, novellas or short stories.

We'll discuss stuff like that later, but realise you want to separate these lists. The reason for the separation is simple – you get different levels of open rates. You want to safeguard organic lists with your life, whereas the other is more likely to have individuals who are (overall) less interested in you. Check out Tammy

Lebrecque's book, Newsletter Ninja: How to Become an Author Mailing List Expert, for more information.

A Social Media Account

If you're a beginning author, realise that the vast majority of the time, spending money to promote your work is going to be a negative return on investment (ROI). There are ways around that (AMS can be good at that); but in general, without multiple books and multiple books in a series, you're going to be losing more money advertising. In that sense, building a social media account and interacting like a consumer of the social media with potential fans will be the cheapest and most cost-effective manner.

I don't mention which social media site to use for two reasons: your personal inclinations are important. If you use Facebook, that's where I'd point you at. If you use Reddit, the same. Where your target market hangs out. This might not be the same as above, though you'll find quite often with the larger social media systems, that there will be groups. The size of those groups will vary.

Example – I really don't think there's a huge LitRPG group in Pinterest. I might be wrong… but I doubt it.

One thing to consider is to look up the demographics of each group. Pinterest leans more towards women, Facebook these days is filled with older people and TikTok is where the young and cool are right now. In either case, remember to be part of the community first, join the various subreddits, Facebook groups, Twitter conversations, etc. as a regular part of the community before you begin advertising. Being genuine will make your social media promoting work much better rather than running in and dropping a post. That's a VERY good way to get yourself banned.

Amazon AuthorCentral

Yes, yes, Amazon is evil and a monopoly, etc. But it's still a good idea to make sure you claim your own books on Amazon AuthorCentral and make sure all your books are set up there. It's also useful to keep an eye on your books and make sure they are all listed as a series and all your paperbacks, hardcovers and audiobooks are linked. All this can be done via e-mails to the contact form or via their new series page formatter in your author account.

And that's it. Those are the basic tools. Later on, you'll want to start looking at advertising, which we'll talk about. However, if you're just starting out, the above is the minimum I'd recommend you start with.

More Advanced Promotional Options

I'm going to start naming a few other tools I make use of and the various main promotional options. I'll cover each briefly, but realise that most of these require a significant amount of time to get right. Again, remember, each promotional center below will touch people at different areas in the sales funnel, so figuring out where and when would be good. Let's start with some of the most common.

Amazon Marketing Services (AMS)

This is where AMS ads will show sponsored search results of your book/series when people are browsing on Amazon itself. This means you're touching people at the lowest level of the funnel possible (before they hit 'buy' on your product), so it can be very, very effective. For those who have used Google Adwords, the basic set-up is similar for their sponsored search. You have two major options when you create a sponsored search result. You can use an automated advertisement, where Amazon will fill in keywords and searches for you or you can enter keywords/ASINs/categories manually.

To start, I would recommend using an automated advertisement, keeping track of sales and spend and then moving the 'good' keywords over to a manual advertisement. Note that there's a significant lag, and it can take Amazon multiple days to push up sales, so it's worth being patient. This is a very, very basic recommendation; and there are multiple good courses (Mark Dawson, Dave Chesson, etc.) who I'd recommend you research taking.

If you do decide to go manual, places to find keywords include your own market research, also-boughts (from your product and also competitors) and some of the automated services out there. You'll need to keep a close eye on your budget and your spend, at least in the beginning as manual advertising can often burn through your funds faster than you'd expect with minimal sales.

Things to note about AMS:

- It works best if you are already selling (in my experience)
- You need a good cover and hopefully, a decent blurb to get the most out of it.
- AMS will relate sales that happen up to 14 days after your advertisement is clicked. That is, if someone buys your book 14 days after they clicked on your ad, it will still count towards your sales data.
- ACOS (Advertising Cost of Sales) is based off Amazon top-line revenue. That is, off the retail price of your book

(e.g. $4.99) and not the royalty rate paid to you (i.e. the 70% of the above $4.99). This means that you will have to manually discount the amount and revenue sold to reach an estimate of what you earned.

I'm not going to go into AMS much more since I am not an expert on it. I do okay, but I have the hardest time making Amazon take my money. My ROI is positive, but I can't spend as much as I want. Which might be a testament to how narrow my keywords have become as I found the ones that work for me.

Facebook Advertising

Facebook advertising is really, really useful for a vast majority of writers. It can also eat your capital without blinking and return nothing. To do Facebook Advertising right, you need to make sure your targeting is very, very good. However, many six figure and more authors have found great success on Facebook.

Some ways to help make your targeting better:
- Put a tracking pixel on your website. That will track people who are coming to your website and add them to a list of potential targets. You don't have access to individual names, etc. but the data is stored as a sample that you can target directly.

- Create a Facebook Fan Page (for yourself as an Author). Those who 'like' your fan page can be targeted directly.
- Your newsletter e-mail addresses can also be used to create another set of audience members.

Now, in most cases, what you'll want to do is create what Facebook calls a 'lookalike' audience. That is, you take any of the above audiences (or more, there are a lot more ways of getting audiences not listed here) and have Facebook create a lookalike audience. This will expand the audience to a million or two, if you have the right numbers.

After that, it's all about testing. What do you test?

- Which lookalike audience interacts the most with your ads
- Which ad copy and ad design works best
- Which landing page will get you the most sales
- Which landing page/book will get you the most read-through (not necessarily the same thing as above)
- And more. You can test and develop a ton of things, with Facebook.

Obviously, this works if your audience is on FB; but it's large enough that it likely is.

Newsletter Lists

I mentioned before that you can get new newsletter subscribers via newsletter services like Bookfunnel and StoryOrigin. There are also dedicated websites that send out newsletters to readers who are looking for a deal. Bookbub is by far the most famous, though other sites include Book Barbarian, FreeBooksy, eReader News Today, etc.

Which one is most effective would depend on your genre and if you are doing full price, promotional pricing or free. Also, which one is most effective at this time will change, so do your research and be willing to test them out over a period of time.

However, all that said, these can definitely provide a boost in sales that will, hopefully, also generate a boost in readthrough (and thus profits).

Other Promotional Tools

Alright, now we've tackled the most common and, in many ways the most effective, promotional tactics that indie authors use. Now, I'm going to list and discuss some more generic websites and other types of promotional tools.

Search Engine Marketing (SEM)

In terms of SEM, there are two major areas – getting good Search Engine Rankings on Pages (SERPs) or paid advertising (Google Adwords, etc.).

Google Adwords is another money killer. I've not heard of any major (i.e. 6 figure author) be a big proponent of it. I know, from my own experience, that it is often quite expensive. The biggest issue with Adwords is that you cannot track sales direct when you send over, so you can't tell if something is converting.

Now, if you had a website that sold your products (i.e. you were wide and set up an ecommerce store) and had links, this might work. However, I've not tested this yet and don't know of any authors who have done so – and talked of the great results. Adwords will eat your capital up and is even more finicky than Facebook Ads. I would be very, very careful about touching this.

For getting good SERPs, you need to start doing Search Engine Optimisation. I've written about that before on my blog, but the basic idea is that it is not worth the amount of time most authors would need to spend to get a good result, especially for competitive keyword.

To rank for your own author name, unless you have an extremely common name or one co-owned by someone famous, you should be able to rank for it with minimal effort (especially if it's Jaden Smith Author). For other competitive keywords like 'fantasy' or 'romance', you have almost no chance without significant investment.

I might be rather dismissive about it, and that's mostly because unless you are gearing your entire strategy around developing a blogging/website platform, the amount of time you'll need to develop a good website to rank would (in my experience and view) be better spent **writing**.

Mass Media Paid Advertising

In general, the answer is no. You're welcome to check the cost, but even at the lowest levels – and you can look at books like Guerilla Marketing to figure out how to lower your cost – the cost is prohibitive for most beginning authors. It's worth noting, it's not just the cost of the paid advertisement, but the cost of the creatives and the time finding the right locations and negotiating yourself a placement.

On top of that, it's worth considering your demographics. Many mass media advertising is not targeted enough, so you'll be 'wasting' a lot of funds when you do this. The small caveat I might have is magazines, as some are very specific in their demographics and topics. For example, a gun magazine for a high action, very well written and research action book. Or maybe a history magazine for a historic fiction work. Etc.

Youtube & Book Trailers

Youtube channels take forever to build out. They can be nice secondary source of income (via advertising when you reach the threshold to become a partner), and if you are inclined to this, you can generate some fans. The biggest issue here, like with book blogging and the like, is consistency. For Book Trailers, I've yet to see anyone do really, really well at this. Again, the time taken and the cost generally do not pay back. This might change depending on your demographic, which is why research is worthwhile. But, in general – just no.

Public Relations

I'm categorising book reviews in large newspaper, book bloggers on the internet, YouTube book reviewers and news appearances under this. I'm also including book tours, bookstore visits, school visits and readings, etc. in this.

On a strategic standpoint, Public Relations (PR) can both generate a significant amount of buzz (worth more than the equivalent in paid advertising for your time spent) and have greater impact. However, for the most part, PR is about generating awareness at the top-end of the sales funnel. It will not, for the most part, generate sales immediately.

Brandon Sanderson in his publishing YouTube series discussed how, in *his* book visit where there were 2000 people coming for the signing, maybe 10% would buy a new book from the store. That means 200 new sales (at best). Counter-balanced against that is the expenses of the visit, hotel fees, assistants, time taken for travel, etc.

The point of PR is not to generate sales, but to generate awareness and long-term fans. So, while I'd add it to any toolbox, understand that this is something that needs to be done on a consistent and regular basis, but not with the expectation of immediate growth or change in sales. For PR, the most important aspect is that what you pitch should be NEWS (New, Exciting, Weird or Sex). If you angle your pitch around any of those things, it often helps to convince editors and journalists. Side note about generating PR – you will often find that local newspapers, bookstores, etc. will be much more open to local authors. In addition, there is a secondary effect of having generated a high local presence, over and above sales, in that it opens you to new funding sources – grants, membership on boards or grant committees, school visits, etc.

Awards

A short note about awards. They can be very useful for social proof. I'd recommend doing so, if you can, but do research that such awards have some meaning. There are a ton of 'scam' awards that are more 'pay to play' and have almost no recognition.

I would further point out that anecdotal evidence by those who have won 'big' awards (like the Hugos, Nebulas, etc.) that they often see low to minimal increase in sales due to the winning of the award. The effect might come further down the road as further social proof and on-page/in-hand conversion rates (if said awards are promoted); but direct correlation to sales are low.

This is, by the way the same for bestseller tags like 'USA Today bestseller' or 'New York Times bestseller'. They are useful social proof, but will not, in itself, increase sales of your work.

Conventions, Farmer Markets & other In-Person Sales

Generally, these can be useful for generating a small amount of sales and a low-level of familiarity and income. Again, like many things, repetition often helps.

Realise that in-person sales is a skillset that must be learnt and built. You'll need to work on your booth/table, merchandise properly, be 'on' and friendly and work your pitch and sales technique to generate the best return. In turn, you'll often only find that your daily sales are in the low single or double digits initially. It might never go more than that.

Whether it's better to be writing (or relaxing); is up to you. It can often be easier to build real fans (as people put a face to the author); though again, this might not be something you choose to do. It is viable, but it is a lot of work. And if you are looking at conventions outside your hometown, the direct sales return is often not there.

We have now covered the basics of the most common promotional strategies. Note that this is mostly a strategic discussion, so getting deep into the weeds of specific websites or locations is not my intention, here.

All this information is great, but how do you build your promotional and marketing plan? Well, here it is in brief.

Promotional Plan Development Steps

Decide what your promotional plan looks like in terms of the sales funnel and awareness with reference to your brand and business objective. This might mean taking out author interviews if you are focusing on your work, or adding that in. This might mean looking at beginning to build a newsletter list early because you are looking to launch regularly and need a way to drive Advanced Reviews, etc.

Build your promotional calendar around releases. As an author, your biggest promotional months will be when you have a release. Those are the first things you should plug in.

Input your minimum promotional work with the tools you have (website posts, social media post, newsletter mailings, etc.) into the calendar. Some of this might not need to be recorded if you are going to be doing this regularly and are able to handle the workload. But, if this is the first time you're building out the calendar, it's useful to input all the different ways you're already marketing.

This can also make you think about what works or isn't working if you're an experienced author. If you spend 90% of your time on Twitter but aren't seeing anything happening in terms of sales, perhaps you should consider shifting your time allocation to some other social media or just adjusting how you interact.

Work out what additional promotional tools you intend to use, weighing what capital you have to spend. When thinking of capital used, consider it both in terms of **money and time you spend.** This includes the amount of time you spend learning how to do social media or joining a community or working out how AMS works, etc. Remember, you are an author. Writing the next book is often your best marketing for your other books.

Add this to your promotional calendar, working out the when and how. Add sales promotions (see pricing) on top of that. Often, adding sales promotions to a newsletter blast or a FB marketing campaign can boost the conversion rates and elicit interest. Planning when you are doing these sales promotions (during non-launch months, etc) can also smooth out your revenue and keep interest in your work high.

Revise the calendar when you realise you either spent too much or are committing to too much work. I'm not joking. You'll find you want to do everything. You can't. Especially if you are learning something new (like Facebook, or how to build a website, etc.). Try to only schedule one new thing a quarter unless you're very experienced.

Print or reference work as the year goes along, recording what works and what doesn't. Remember, it's always good to have goals that you can track and record against. Not knowing if what you are doing is working or not can be really tough.

Revise the calendar when required as results come in if necessary. I'd look at it every 3 months or so for a revision. Maybe more or less as your writing schedule changes too.

Examples

Alright, we did a ton of theory, but let's talk a few examples.

Bob

We'll call example one, Bob. Bob wants to write a book. He's not sure he ever wants to write more than one, it's kind of a bucket list item. He's thinking what he'd like to write a biography of his grandfather or perhaps, a full historical war novel around World War II. Realistically, Bob's not sure he'll ever do more than a single book. He's written most of the work based off his grandfather's stories, but he's not certain how well written the work is, since this is his first attempt.

In this sense, Bob's not a career writer. Not yet. His dream isn't to make a living out of writing, but to see his book published. He'd prefer a bookstore, but he's open to the idea of indie publishing. When asked about timeline, Bob's uncertain. He doesn't have a need to get this work done soon, his grandfather is still healthy and able to answer further question, though Bob would prefer the work to be released before his grandfather passes. In that sense, faster is better. Knowing that, Bob can begin working his career and marketing plan.

First, he decides that he'd rather have it released faster than wait for an agent and go trad pub. He'd need to do a lot more work, and he's still not sure of the focus of his book. So, he has to figure out his product.

Research shows there's more of a market for historical war fiction than a memoir, so he decides to shift the book in that direction. He decides that he's too new to really know how to write the book properly, so he knows he'll have to get the full suite of editors. Since he's paying for at least a developmental editor to assuage his personal concerns, he figures there's no point looking for a small publisher who might take him on. He just doesn't have a product ready for them and by the time he does, he'd have spent a large portion of his budget anyway.

In terms of product types, well, he wants a hardcover edition for his own personal use. A paperback seems a decent option and maybe large print for his grandfather. All that will cost money (or time) to do the formatting, so he starts doing estimates of cost on top of that. Audiobooks are put aside though, since he knows his budget is going to be eaten up by editing.

When it comes to pricing, Bob wants to break even more than anything else. In that sense, he decides he's going to go in with a higher base price, put it on KU since that'll let him sell it 'cheap' at the same time. Adding the paperbacks that he'll have created, he feels it'll definitely anchor the price better.

Distribution wise, since he's going with Kindle Unlimited and Amazon, Bob's pretty set. He needs to use a PoD printer, like Ingram Sparks, but that's not a major issue and Bob knows that he'll probably not sell a lot of books. The Large Print edition isn't likely to sell much either, but that's for his grandfather so it's a cost he's willing to bear even if it makes no business sense. He also likes the idea of KU and being Amazon exclusive since he doesn't want the hassle of managing multiple accounts. Having one account to worry about for the most part works for him since he has to do all this in-between his full-time career.

That just leaves promotional strategies. Building a website seems a lot of hassle for one book, so he decides to skip that. Bob still uses Facebook, so he doesn't mind creating a FB Author page and getting an Amazon Author account. A mailing list seems to be more work than he's willing to do and he figures it's only useful for future books he will not release. So, he's chosen to skip that for now.

He knows he could get people on his mailing list, but he has a large number of friends which he'll just bother instead. It's not the best option, but it's easy enough for him to do and Bob's a sociable person anyway. Along with joining FB groups and posting on the various forums about world war 2 history that he joined while researching the book, he figures that'll be a decent platform to being promoting.

Bob glances at the other promotional options for spending money and decides he doesn't want to spend the time learning various other marketing platforms. It's too much work and he just doesn't care.

After writing it down, Bob's got a rough idea of what he's going to do. It's not the most robust of marketing plans, but it works for him. He gets back to writing, hoping that everything he's done will help sell some books and recover his cost.

Now, remember, Bob's main goal isn't to make money (though breaking even would be nice). It's to have a published book he can point at and say '*I did this*'. In that sense, Bob's willing to spend money and come out at a loss which is why he's compromising on so many portions of the promotional aspects.

And that's one example. If Bob had more confidence in his writing, he might instead try shopping his work out to a small publisher. They would take over the editing and promotion process, with Bob having a much lower royalty rate. This might even be the 'better' option financially, especially since Bob doesn't care about making money. His issue is what most writers have – lack of confidence in his work. In Bob's case, this might be true due to his lack of experience. It's hard to say for sure since this is just a made-up example. But here's two different paths for the same person.

Sue

We talked about Bob in the previous example who might end up going trad pub since he's not that interested in building a career. But let's talk about Sue next.

Sue's a little different from Bob. She's a housewife, takes care of her kids and loves writing; but isn't sure if she wants to become a full-time author. It'd be nice, but she knows it's really tough. On the other hand, she has some time to do writing when the kids are at school and if she earned some pin money, that'd be great.

Sue looks into trad publishing. She'd have to get an agent unless she went with a small press who take unsolicited works. Since she writes romance, she also does more research and finds out that a lot of the market has moved online to e-books. Further research shows that there are a ton of forums, reader groups and people willing to talk about new author works. What surprises her even more is how many great premade covers for cheap that she finds. She even finds a small writing group that meet during the day. It's perfect for her to get out of the house, meet new people and trade writing tips and editing.

She doesn't have a huge budget, but she figures she can swing a premade cover and proofreading every few months from her personal savings. Add in the editing help from her new friends at the writing group, and while it won't be perfect, it'll be better than nothing.

Knowing all that, Sue decides to go indie publishing. Product wise, she has that worked out in terms of editing, proofreading and cover. It won't be the best, but it's an adequate level – a minimum viable product. She also wants to write the small-town romances she loves to read – and maybe put a little authenticity to it since she actually lives in a small town. She doesn't think she'll have the money to do audiobooks, so she resolves to throw it up for royalty share on ACX and see if she can get any nibbles that way. Otherwise, paperback sounds fun to have but she doesn't have the budget for it.

Writing wise, she knows she can confidently release once every six months, maybe once every three months. So she'll plan for that. It isn't going to be every month, so she's going to have to do promos around that. Thinking about promotions, beyond joining the various social groups, she wants to build an author brand and showcase her own hometown which is incredibly proud of and feels is extremely beautiful. She plans to launch an Instagram, TikTok and YouTube channel at the same time, just to show people around and talk of her life and how it affects her writing. She figures she can do it while taking the kids out for a walk on the weekends.

As for distribution, she is not sure. Going wide has some appeal to get international markets, who might be interested in small town life in the US from her other social media channels, but KU means she only needs to worry about one area. For now, she's putting a pin in that, but figures she could launch with KU to start, and if she doesn't do well, take the book wide after the three month exclusivity is over. It's possible that she might do that for every new release, giving her the best of both worlds.

Pricing wise, she knows she'll need to start cheap as a new writer. She's also not confident her writing is that good yet – her writing group says its fine, but rough – so she'll price at $2.99 for now. Once she does better, she'll increase the price. She also bookmarks the idea of a permafree book and a short story introduction, both for the future. If she has time or comes up with an idea, she might try to send out short stories to various magazines as another promotional method.

The biggest goal is to release cheap and as often as possible. If she can get books out cheaply, with minimal cost, she figures she can slowly build up her audience. Sue's in no rush, her kids are in school for a decade plus more and her husband has a great job. She can afford to take her time, build her craft and hopefully, an audience.

She'll revise her ideas once she has more books out and knows how her sales have been.

Manjit

We've done a couple of new writers, but let's tackle an experienced writer. We'll call him Manjit.

Manjit has six books released in two different series, one series with four books and the other with two. He's done okay for himself in Kindle Unlimited and baseline gets a few hundred dollars a month with release months getting him a thousand to two thousand on launch. He's not done a lot of publicity though, most of his marketing has been to his readers who have found him via 'also boughts' and browsing the categories. Still, he's done better than he could ever expect and wants to make a go at being full-time. That means he needs to make a couple of thousand dollars a month regularly which will allow him to pay for his editors and covers and his rent.

Knowing that, he needs a real marketing strategy.

He takes a look around his genre (Military Sci-fi) and decides there's still a good market in it. He isn't a bestselling author, but he served and his slice of life Military Sci-fi book, which focused on infantry members in an alien world, does okay. He's got great read-through for his best-selling series (of four books) and figures he can keep adding to it. His other series (of two books) is an off-shoot in the same universe.

Manjit decides he can keep writing in the same universe, adding to the main series and the universe, with multiple jump-in points. He has an idea for a Military Police series to delve a little into the law and crime aspects of serving, and another for something a little more action oriented. He's got a great series of products, but since he only has four books in the main series, he figures he'll focus promotion on that rather than the other two book series. He'll get a third book on that and begin marketing that while launching his third, related series. He's a fast writer and gets a book out every 2 months, so it won't take long at all.

Unfortunately, he doesn't have the money to make audiobooks. He doesn't want to do royalty share, but considering he wants to go full-time earlier than later, he decides to take the offer from an audiobook producing company to record his main series. With the money they give him as an advance, he will record the other two book series so that all his work is in audio and reaches more people.

He's been talking to some other authors and he figures he'll use the money he has now and get paperback and hardcover versions of all his work done. He's also going to invest in some stock and spend time pitching his books at flea markets, farmer markets and conventions. That'll increase his distribution options and since he works as a salesperson during his day job, he has no issue with sales at such conventions. In fact, he relishes the thought of talking to people.

Now, for pricing, he plans to try using a loss leader for book 1 in his series. He's going to reduce book 1 to $0.99 for both series and keep it there. That'll lower the barrier to entry and increase the total number of his readers. Since he expects to have multiple series, he believes that having multiple series at $0.99 for people to 'try' will give him more points of entry. That will be helped by having them all listed in slightly different Sci-Fi categories.

At the same time, he intends to go wide. Part of that is because where he lives, KU is not available, but he also wants an international audience. Americans seem to have an issue with his use of British spelling so he figures he'll just double down on expanding wide. In addition, the fact that 'wide' income seems more stable is very important to him. He does know that he'll lose some of his Kindle Unlimited income in the short term and that going 'wide' takes a while, but stability is more important than speed for Manjit.

Knowing that he's going 'wide', Manjit intends to use a lot of Facebook and promotional newsletter advertising. He also thinks he has a chance to get onto some panels and blogs, so he'll spend time writing news releases and inquiries to various bloggers and papers. He has a friend who works as a journalist who's willing to help him with all the public relations outreach and might even get him an article in the newspaper.

Promotional free pricing with the various newsletter promos will be important to him, as well as building up his newsletter list. Both of those are high on his list, though he doesn't have time to build the newsletter list too much, so he figures he'll spend his time on paid newsletter promos for now. He plans on trying AMS, but he'll keep his budget very, very low. He might even kill it if he can't make it work. AMS, for Manjit, is going to be his 10% off the wall spend.

For Manjit, the focus will be building up a stable source of income. That means getting himself out to as many retailers and distributors as he can. He can't afford to have huge swings up and down, as his own responsibilities are much more fixed. Wide distribution is the way Manjit figures he'll do this, with fast and rapid release of books to build his backlist. Having multiple points of entry into his universe will also aid him as it'll give him more opportunities to hit the elusive Bookbub feature.

In the meantime, he figures he'll see if he can build up some local/regional notoriety. If he can supplement his income with talks/craft workshops/in-person sales, that would be a bonus.

Xiu Li

As one final example of the way you can use the information within to develop a marketing strategy, we'll talk about Xiu Li.

Xiu Li is a traditionally published young adult author who managed to be signed by a traditional publisher, but the publisher subsequently dropped her due to low (for them) sales. She managed to sell just over 3000 copies, which unfortunately wasn't sufficient for her publisher to keep her on for the rest of the trilogy.

Now, having dealt with the disappointment and having no luck in the last few years shopping around a new series, Xiu Li decides that it's time to indie publish. She's got a few things she needs to consider.

First, she starts reviewing her contract with her publishing house to find out whether she can indie publish the remainder of her original trilogy. If she can do that, at least she won't disappoint her fans. It looks like she should be able to get her rights reverted for the unpublished sequels, but she needs to make the request and send some letters to trigger the revision process with her publisher.

Next, because she has this other trilogy written and ready to go, she is trying to decide what to do about it. She's not sure she can do the indie author thing of releasing quickly, but she does have this trilogy all written already and she is halfway through in writing another trilogy.

Realising she's a 'slow' writer compared to most indie authors, she decides her best bet is to rapid release her trilogies rather than releasing them as she finishes. It'll be more expensive in total, but she likes the ability to adjust her books once she finishes the entire series arc, so she resolves to do this.

Financially, she has a number of author friends, some who are willing to trade editing and proofreading services. This will keep the cost of her editing down, allowing her to spend on things like a final proofread and a nice (expensive) on-genre cover. She plans to keep an eye out for cover auctions and sales, since she has a bit of time.

In terms of distribution and pricing, she is vacillating between Kindle Unlimited and going wide. Due to her previous trad pub contract, she knows she has 'wide' fans, many of whom might have picked up her work in print. However, doing PoD means it will be expensive to get books out at a low enough price for them. After some thought, Xiu Li decides to try to crowdfund a printrun for the remainder two books. If that works, she can provide paperbacks at a lower cost, get them into bookstores that might still be interested, sell e-books and throw them up on other retailers for those who missed it.

Luckily, she's kept all the contact information of the people who interviewed her during the launch of her first book, and she believes she can get a few more interviews and reviews from book bloggers for the next few books too when she is ready to release.

If her Kickstarter works, Xiu Li decides she'll stay wide and keep e-book pricing slightly higher than 'normal' indies in the hope of keeping the same 'prestige' factor as her other trad pub authors. That means around $5.99 or $6.99 per book. After all, she's already made her money back from the Kickstarter, so everything else she earns will be pure profit.

In the meantime, she'll get her 3rd series written, her 2nd series edited and proofread and find covers for it all so that she's ready to release. If she plans this right, she might even be able to release eight books in a period of a year to two years.

After that, it'll be a bit before she can release any further work, but she'll try to work on writing faster.

Afterword

This work is my basic attempt at providing context to an author trying to navigate their career and developing their author brand. As mentioned at the start, much of marketing theory is – in my view – not a step-by-step guide, but a framework of thought. Use that framework to help guide your thinking, develop goals and return to your marketing plan regularly to update as both the external environment and your own career changes.

Understand that being an author can be a long term career, one that requires a significant amount of time to establish and prosper within. However, changes in the publishing system, in the development of technology has made it possible for a larger number of authors than ever.

Technology and distribution methods for authors continue to expand. Opportunities continue to expand and, in some cases, close out. At the same time, there are numerous individuals and corporations attempting to prey upon new authors, with predatory contracts (always get a lawyer to read over your contract before signing!) and workshops that provide little additional information.

However, the truth is that success in publishing is as much as factor of persistence as it is luck. Not every book, not every series will be a success. It might take multiple books and series before you find a genre and an audience that will work for you. Even as an established author, I have released books that are 'flops' (fewer than a thousand sales after the first month).

Persistence, luck and a willingness to continually learn will aid you in progressing your career. A marketing strategy will help decrease the weighting that luck will have on your career, but it can and will always be a factor.

Lastly, while I have said this before, I want to reiterate. While this work is based upon marketing strategy development, as an author – as an artist – your ultimate level of success will depend on your work. The product – how well written it is – will dictate if you manage to make fans. While work that is not well-written can sell, a minimum level of quality is required for an on-going career.

If you've enjoyed what you've read, if you want more details, do note that I have an on-going, weekly post on my site about the business aspects of writing. This includes ruminations about previous years, examples of sales and marketing tactics tested (often with numbers generated from my own books) and more. Feel free to browse it for free at: mylifemytao.com or to visit my Patreon where posts appear in advance.

Further Reading

In this section, I have compiled a list of helpful resources which cover both generic business topics and topics that are specific to publishing.

Before you read this though, realise that I have a general business degree and a marketing degree. I also ran a business for 12 years. I have read a LOT of books, many of whom were just meh to me – because they reiterated what I knew with a nugget of information inside – while others that are good (e.g. Blue Ocean Strategy) are less useful for authors.

I built my business scaffolding over two decades, so this list is by no means exhaustive. I sometimes can't see the water I swim in. That being said, this list should give you an excellent start.

Business Resources

- If you are running a business and looking to expand, The E-Myth Revisited by Michael E. Gerber is very helpful.
- The Harvard Business Review Book for New Managers will help you learn the basics of business, leadership, and how to read a financial statement.

Contracts & Scams

- Closing the Deal on Your Terms by Kristine Kathryn Rusch has to do with dealbreakers in contracts that crop up. It is a very good primer on things to watch out for.
- The [Writer's Beware](#) blog provides information on up-to-date scams. Always check here before you do a deal with a publisher. Also, ask around – but check here first!
- The [Writer's Beware](#) website contains common schemes & scams, as well as generic information to read and understand.

Copyright

- The Copyright Handboook: What Every Writer Needs to Know by Stephen Fishman. Read it. Understand it. Use it.
- The Writer Got Screwed (but didn't have to be) by Brooke A. Wharton is very screenwriting/ Hollywood focused. Also, I found it very basic. But if you're just starting out, this can be quite useful as it is an easier read than above, covers some copyright stuff and contract things. **It is dated so read with care**.

Advertising (Generic)

- Hey, Whipple, Squeeze This by Luke Sullivan is about ads but… guess what? Your cover is an ad. Read this to understand the basics of what a good ad is and the kind of things you need to think about.
- The Copywriter's Handbook by Robert W. Bly focuses on how to write copy. Like, for your blurbs?

You should combine the above copywriting book with one geared towards online copywriting. Check around for online sites via Google. The above book has some information, but I found the online sites (especially those with how-to guides for long, one-page copy) are better. Sadly, I don't have those resources bookmarked anymore.

Author Advertising (Specific)

- Help! My Facebook Ads Suck by Michael Cooper and Mal Cooper is a great beginner work. It's cheap, easy to read and if you have used FB ads before, probably nothing new. But some interesting tips and great for beginners.
- Newsletter Ninja by Tammi L. Labrecque
- AMS (Amazon Marketing Services): Mark Dawson's course is super popular. I haven't done it so I can't personally recommend it, but there's probably a good

reason he's so popular. Felicia Beasely has a course, which I've taken. I've listened to her speak, and she's good, but the course is expensive.

Authors with Book Series that I think You Should Read

- Successful Indie Author by Craig Martelle is a great series if you're starting out. I particularly got a lot of use from his discussion on collaborations because I never had to deal with that previously. Other stuff (like pricing) was less useful, but I run my own tests. Generally, worth reading.
- The Three-year, No-bestseller Plan For Making a Sustainable Living From Your Fiction by Patty Jensen. Patty writes and distributes wide. Because of that, her viewpoint is different. If you're going wide, it's worth reading over.
- WMG Writer's Guide Series are books written by Kristine Kathryn Rusch and Dean Wesley Smith. Much of the content in these books is available for free on both of their respective websites, but the books are more complex in form. I recommend reading both sites for on-going information.

Generic Author Sites & Groups

- Kboards – The Writer's Café (a subforum in kboards) used to be more useful, but lots of answers to questions, editors, proofers cover artists offering services, etc.

- 20Booksto50k Group – Probably the best and most informative group. There are regularly posts with great information. Just temper your expectations when you see successes – sometimes, you won't be part of those. Also… consider if the recommendations work for you. As they say, there are multiple paths up the mountain. Choose yours and use what you can.

- Wide for the Win Facebook Group – If you're going wide, this is the group to join. There is so much information, with actual details and people reporting back on results.

- 6 Figure Authors – More podcast than site, but well worth checking in on.

- Kriswrites – Kristyn Kathryn Rusch's Business Blog has been going on for years and has a TON of great information. Understand that she and Dean Wesley Smith have very clear and strong beliefs, Some, I disagree with. But realise they are also authors who have been writing for over 30 years, full-time, so there is legitimate success (both awards and in a long-spanning, full-time career) here.

- [Chris Fox's videos on writing](#)
- [The Creative Penn](#) – Joanna Penn's writing business resources

About the Author

Tao Wong is an avid fantasy and sci-fi reader who spends his time working and writing in the North of Canada. He's spent way too many years doing martial arts of many forms and, having broken himself too often, now spends his time writing about fantasy worlds. He used to run one of the largest game stores in Canada, worked as the marketing manager for a number of companies and now spends his time writing.

If you'd like to support Tao directly, he has a Patreon page where previews of all his new books can be found!

Tao Wong's Patreon: https://www.patreon.com/taowong

For updates on the series and the author's other books (and special one-shot stories), please visit his website: http://www.mylifemytao.com

Subscribers to Tao's mailing list will receive exclusive access to short stories in the Thousand Li and System Apocalypse universes: https://www.subscribepage.com/taowong

Or visit his Facebook Page:
https://www.facebook.com/taowongauthor/

About the Publisher

Starlit Publishing is wholly owned and operated by Tao Wong. It is a science fiction and fantasy publisher focused on the LitRPG & cultivation genres. Their focus is on promoting new, upcoming authors in the genre whose writing challenges the existing stereotypes while giving a rip-roaring good read.

For more information on Starlit Publishing, visit our website: https://www.starlitpublishing.com/

You can also join Starlit Publishing's mailing list to learn of new, exciting authors and book releases.

https://starlitpublishing.com/newsletter-signup/

www.ingramcontent.com/pod-product-compliance
Lightning Source LLC
Chambersburg PA
CBHW021447070526
44577CB00002B/292